Learn Every Day About Our Green Earth

Edited by Kathy Charner

Learn Every Day
About OUR GREEN EARTH

100 BEST IDEAS from TEACHERS

EDITED BY
Kathy Charner

© 2010 Gryphon House, Inc.
Published by Gryphon House, Inc.
10770 Columbia Pike, Suite 201
Silver Spring, MD 20901
800.638.0928; 301.595.9500; 301.595.0051 (fax)

Visit us on the web at www.gryphonhouse.com

Illustrations: Deb Johnson

Library of Congress Cataloging-in-Publication Information:
Learn every day about our green earth / edited by Kathy Charner.
    p. cm.
ISBN 978-0-87659-127-7
1. Earth—Juvenile literature. I. Charner, Kathy.
QB631.4.L43 2010
372.35'7—dc22
                                    2009051771

BULK PURCHASE

Gryphon House books are available for special premiums and sales promotions as well as for fund-raising use. Special editions or book excerpts also can be created to specification. For details, contact the Director of Marketing at Gryphon House.

DISCLAIMER

Gryphon House, Inc. and the author cannot be held responsible for damage, mishap, or injury incurred during the use of or because of activities in this book. Appropriate and reasonable caution and adult supervision of children involved in activities and corresponding to the age and capability of each child involved is recommended at all times. Do not leave children unattended at any time. Observe safety and caution at all times.

Table of Contents

Note: The books listed in the Related Children's Books section of each activity may occasionally include books that are only available used or through your local library.

Introduction

You have in your hands a great teacher resource! This book, which is part of the Learn Every Day series, contains 100 activities you can use with children ages 3–6 to help them develop a lifelong love of learning, as well as the knowledge and skills all children need to become successful students in kindergarten and beyond. The activities in this book are written by teachers and professionals from the field of early childhood education—educators and professionals who use these activities in their classrooms every day.

The activities in this book are separated by curriculum areas, such as Art, Dramatic Play, Outdoor Play, Transitions, and so on, and are organized according to their age appropriateness, so activities appropriate for children ages three and up come first, then activities appropriate for children ages four and up, and finally, activities for children ages five and up. Each activity has the following components—learning objectives, a list of related vocabulary words, a list of thematically related books, a list of the materials (if any) you need to complete the activity, directions for preparation and the activity itself. Also included in each activity is an assessment component to help you observe how well the children are meeting the learning objectives. Given the emphasis on accountability in early childhood education, these assessment strategies are essential.

Several activities also contain teacher-to-teacher tips that provide smart and useful ideas, including how to expand the central idea of an activity in a new way or where to find the materials necessary to complete a given activity. Some activities also include related fingerplays, poems, or songs that you can sing and chant with the children. Children love singing, dancing, and chanting. These actions that help expand children's understanding of an activity's learning objectives.

This book, and the other books in this series, give early childhood educators 100 great activities that require few materials, little if any preparation, and are sure to make learning fun and engaging for children.

Nature Brushes

3+

LEARNING OBJECTIVES

The children will:
1. Develop their small motor skills.
2. Explore paint and painting.

Materials

feathers
pine needles
sticks
watercolor paint
   (in solid cakes)
water
white paper

VOCABULARY

feather	needle	pine
leaf	painting	stick

WHAT TO DO

1. Discuss painting with the children. Explain that people often use brushes to paint, but it is possible to use a wide variety of materials when making a painting.
2. Place feathers, pine needles, leaves, and sticks within the children's reach.
3. Give each child a paper and watercolors.
4. Invite the children to use the items on the table or an easel to paint a picture.
5. Encourage the children to paint scenes they see, or to imagine scenes or abstract designs they would like to paint.
6. Talk with the children about their paintings as they are working. Ask the children to describe what they are painting.

TEACHER-TO-TEACHER TIPS

- Take the children on a nature walk so they can collect the items that they will use to paint with.
- Have the children use other items to paint with, such as kitchen utensils or old tools.

ASSESSMENT

Consider the following:
- How well are the children able to manipulate and use the natural objects as painting tools?
- Are the children engaged? Are they happy with the art they created?
- What do the children choose to paint? Ask them to discuss their work. Consider having a group discussion about everyone's paintings.

Linda S. Andrews, Sonora, CA

Children's Books

The Big Book for Our Planet by Ann Durell
The Earth and I by Frank Asch
Earthdance by Joanne Ryder

Clean Up the Beach!

4+

LEARNING OBJECTIVES

The children will:
1. Talk about ways they can clean up the environment at the beach.
2. Improve their vocabulary.
3. Learn that taking care of the Earth can be fun.

Materials

blue paper
crayons
sand
glue
selection of trash and natural items that may be found in the sand or water at the beach (plastic soda bottles, pieces of crumpled paper, Popsicle™ sticks, plastic water jug lids, straws, snack bags or wrappers, shells, rocks, and starfish)
sand pails

VOCABULARY

clean	litter	rocks	shells	trash
fish	pick up	sand	star	

WHAT TO DO

1. Encourage the children to create a beach scene using blue paper and crayons.
2. Invite the children to display their pictures and tell what they learned about taking care of our world while at the beach. For extra fun have sand and glue available so the children can create a sandy beach picture.
3. Place 10 of the items (include litter, shells, recyclables) in a plastic sand pail. Ask one child to remove each item and tell whether it belongs in the sand at the beach or somewhere else. Have the children explain where each item should go if it doesn't belong in the sand.

SONG

Cleaning Up the Beach by Mary J. Murray
(Tune: "Baby Bumblebee")
I'm cleaning up the beach now, don't you see?
Mom and dad will be so proud of me.
I'm picking up anything I can see.
That doesn't belong in the sand.

ASSESSMENT

Consider the following:
● How well do the children differentiate between what belongs at the beach and what is litter?
● Do the children understand why it is important to have clean beaches?

Mary J. Murray, Mazomanie, WI

Children's Books

I Can Save the Earth! One Little Monster Learns to Reduce, Reuse, and Recycle by Alison Inches
Planet Patrol: A Kids' Action Guide to Earth Care by Marybeth Lorbiecki
Your Environment by Brenda Williams

ART

Collage Treasures

4+

LEARNING OBJECTIVES

The children will:
1. Learn about objects from nature and how the Earth is filled with beautiful things.
2. Appreciate their natural surroundings.
3. Develop early writing skills.

Materials

bags or small
  containers
nature items, such
  as twigs, grasses,
  shells, seeds,
  sand, mud,
  pebbles, acorns,
  and so on
paper
markers
pencils
glue

VOCABULARY

beautiful	collect	nature	scenery
collages	Earth	read	write

WHAT TO DO

1. Discuss with the children how we can take care of the Earth by using things from nature, the same way we recycle, to make beautiful artwork.
2. Give each child a bag or small container for collecting. Take the children outside to collect the objects from nature.
3. After the children have collected their treasures, give each child a large piece of strong paper, glue, and markers.
4. Explain to the children that from their found treasures they will make a treasure collage, a water scene, for example. They can place the objects on the paper to resemble any scene they want. Then the children can dictate or write a little about their creations.

TEACHER-TO-TEACHER TIP

● Encourage the children to share their pictures with each other or the group and then display them.

ASSESSMENT

Consider the following:
● Do the children share details about their pictures with each other? Can they name the objects they collected?
● Are the children able to identify the letters in some of the related words?

Eileen Lucas, Fort McMurray, Alberta, Canada

Children's Books

The Earth and I by
Frank Asch
Taking Care of the Earth
by Billy Goodman
*Taking Care of
Mother Earth* by
Leanne Flett Kruger

Colorful Recycled Paper

4+

LEARNING OBJECTIVES

The children will:
1. Learn about how paper is made and recycled.
2. Develop their small motor skills.

Materials

newspapers
mixing bowl
water
egg beater
measuring cups and
   spoons
2 tablespoons
   cornstarch
food coloring
flat pan
screen (to fit into
   flat pan)

VOCABULARY

newspaper	pulp	stationery
paper	recycle	

WHAT TO DO

1. Ask each child to tear a page of newspaper into tiny bits. Place the bits into a mixing bowl and cover them with water.
2. Allow the paper to soak for an hour.
3. Help the children use an egg beater to beat the paper until it forms a pulp.
4. Mix in cornstarch, one cup of water, and food coloring.
5. Place a screen in the bottom of a flat pan.
6. Pour the pulpy mixture into the pan and let it sit for three minutes.
7. Remove the screen (covered with the mix) and put it on newspaper to dry.
8. Place more newspaper over the top of the screen and press down hard.
9. Remove the top newspaper and let the pulp dry overnight.
10. When it is dry, peel the paper from the screen.
11. Help the children write a note on this recycled stationery!

ASSESSMENT

Consider the following:
● Do the children understand that it is important to recycle paper to help conserve natural resources?
● How well do the children engage in the activity? Do they enjoy the process of pulping the paper?

Lisa M. Chichester, Parkersburg, WV

Children's Books

Earth Day by
Amy Margaret
Earth Day Birthday by
Pattie Schnetzler
Recycle Every Day! by
Nancy Elizabeth
Wallace

Earth Balls

LEARNING OBJECTIVES

The children will:
1. Begin to understand that the Earth is round.
2. Develop social skills as they share materials on a common workspace.

Materials

papier-mâché
   recipe
newspaper
balloons
yarn
paint: brown,
   white, green, and
   blue
paintbrushes

VOCABULARY

bumpy	hill	papier-mâché	smooth
Earth	mountain	round	valley

PAPIER-MÂCHÉ RECIPE

Ingredients: water, flour
- Mix together 1 part flour to 2 parts water to the consistency of runny glue (not thick like paste). Add more water or flour as necessary. Mix well to remove any lumps. Store in an airtight container.

PREPARATION

- Tear newspaper into many pieces.
- Cover the work area with a vinyl tablecloth and place a shallow bowl of papier-mâché mixture and a pile of torn newspaper strips between every two chairs.
- Loosely inflate several small round balloons.

WHAT TO DO

1. Give each child a small, loosely inflated balloon. Show the children how to dip the newspaper strips into the papier-mâché mix and lay them on the balloons.
2. As the children work, point out that their Earth Balls are the same shape as our planet Earth. Point out that papier-mâché is not exactly smooth and neither is the crust of the Earth. The Earth has lots of lumps and bumps, such as hills, mountains, and deep valleys.
3. Tie yarn around the ends of the papier-mâché-covered balloons and hang them up to dry.
4. When they are dry, give the balloons back to the children and ask them to paint the balloons with all the colors of the Earth. Provide brown, white, green, and blue paint and small paintbrushes.
5. Display the completed Earth Balls around the room.

Children's Books

The Earth and I by Frank Asch
Earth Day Birthday by Pattie Schnetzler
The Wump World by Bill Peet

ASSESSMENT

Consider the following:
- Can the children describe similarities between the Earth and their papier-mâché sculptures?
- How well do the children share the materials?

Virginia Jean Herrod, Columbia, SC

Earth Day Play

4+

LEARNING OBJECTIVES

The children will:
1. Develop their small motor skills.
2. Learn about the importance of caring for the Earth.

Materials

large white paper
child-safe scissors
easel
green and blue
　　tempera paint
rocks (one for each
　　child)
paintbrushes
newspaper

VOCABULARY

care	Earth Day	land	sea
Earth	globe	rock	

WHAT TO DO

1. Explain to the children that Earth Day is a day to celebrate our Earth. You can do this activity any day of the year when you want to celebrate the Earth.
2. Ahead of time, cut a huge circle from white paper and place it on an easel. Encourage the children to work cooperatively to paint the "Earth" green and blue. Show them a globe as an inspiration.
3. Go outside and let each child collect a rock. Make baby Earth rocks! Place the rocks on newspaper and encourage the children to paint their rocks blue. Then they can add green spots (land).
4. Talk with the children about how wonderful the Earth is and the different things the children can do to help keep it nice.

Children's Books

The Lorax by Dr. Seuss
Nate the Great Goes Down in the Dumps by Marjorie Weinman Sharmat
Recycle: A Handbook for Kids by Gail Gibbons

ASSESSMENT

Consider the following:
● Do the children work cooperatively to create their Earth replica?
● Do the children indicate an understanding of the importance of caring for the Earth?

Lisa Chichester, Parkersburg, WV

Earth Day Wall Hanging

4+

LEARNING OBJECTIVES

The children will:
1. Learn to work collaboratively.
2. Develop their small motor skills.

Materials

small (6") blue
   paper plates
hole punch
green fingerpaint
   (or green poster
   paint and
   paintbrushes)
8" pieces of yarn
crepe paper
   streamers (blue,
   green, and white)
cellophane tape

VOCABULARY

clouds	land	sky	twist
Earth Day	ocean	streamer	water

WHAT TO DO

1. Give each child a blue 6" paper plate.
2. Punch a hole in the top of each plate and punch three holes spaced out at the bottom. (Double punch the holes to make them larger.)
3. Encourage the children to paint green "land" on the blue "ocean."
4. When the paint has dried, help the children loop and tie yarn through the top hole on their plates. This is the hanger.
5. Give each child one of each color of streamer (blue for water, green for earth, white for the clouds in the sky). Help them thread a different color streamer through each hole along the bottom. It is best to twist one end of each streamer to make it easier.
6. Gently pull about 2" of a streamer through a bottom hole and secure it to the back of the paper plate with cellophane tape.
7. Repeat with the other two streamers.
8. Hang the plates to create an Earth Day wall hanging.

TEACHER-TO-TEACHER TIP

● Talk about recycling. If your school has a recycling program, have each child bring in a clean, empty can to put in the recycling bin.

ASSESSMENT

Consider the following:
● How well do the children work together on this project?
● Are there any specific parts of the project that were difficult for individual children?

Christina R. Chilcote, New Freedom, PA

Children's Books

Earth Day by
Amy Margaret
Earth Day by
David F. Marx
Earth Day Birthday by
Pattie Schnetzler

Flowerpot Boots

4+

LEARNING OBJECTIVES

The children will:
1. Learn how to create something from recycled materials.
2. Learn about art and sculpture.

Materials

items that can be
recycled into
flowerpots, such as
old shoes, boots, or
containers
paint
paintbrushes
decorations, such as
artificial flowers,
yarn, sequins,
feathers, ribbons,
and lace
glue
recyclable items, such
as paper towel
rolls, egg cartons,
boxes, and film
canisters

VOCABULARY

art	dumpster	recycling	trash
create	flowerpot	reuse	
decorate	planter	sculpture	

WHAT TO DO

1. Collect several old shoes or boots you can turn into flowerpots. The children can paint and decorate them to be used in their houses or yards. Mixing paint with glue will add a shiny finish and will keep the paint from chipping off.
2. Have the children bring in scrap decorations such as flowers, yarn, sequins, ribbon, and lace to use for decorating their planter or centerpiece.
3. Another idea is to bring in as many recyclable items as you can find, such as paper towel rolls, egg cartons, boxes, or film canisters and let the children create their own sculpture. You will be surprised at what the children will create.
4. At the end of your project talk about how recycling these items can help protect the Earth and what would happen if we didn't recycle things.

SONG

Play the song "In My Back Yard" from Greg and Steve's CD *Big Fun*.

ASSESSMENT

Consider the following:
- Do the children show that they understand the concept of *reuse*?
- Do the children help build the flowerpot boots?

Children's Books

The Dumpster Diver by
Janet S. Wong
The Great Trash Bash by
Loreen Leedy
*Something from
Nothing* by
Phoebe Gilman

Cookie Zingarelli, Columbus, OH

Stained Glass Globe

LEARNING OBJECTIVES

The children will:
1. Become familiar with using child-safe scissors.
2. Develop their small motor skills.

Materials

white paper
child-safe scissors
blue and green
    markers
cotton balls
vegetable oil

VOCABULARY

beautiful	globe	stained
Earth	land	transparent
environment	plants	water

PREPARATION

● Draw a circle about the size of a paper plate on each piece of paper. Make enough for each child to have one.

WHAT TO DO

1. Explain to the children that taking care of the Earth means taking care of the plants, animals, land, and water. Today the children will make a stained glass globe to hang in a window at home and remind them how beautiful the Earth can be.
2. Give each child a sheet of paper and have them cut out the circle you drew there.
3. Have the children use markers to decorate these globes with green land and blue water.
4. Explain that they will make their paper transparent. Give each child a cotton ball with vegetable oil on it. Have each child rub their drawing gently with the oiled cotton. They can hold up their paper and see through it. Remember to have them wash their hands.

TEACHER-TO-TEACHER TIP

● You will need spray cleaner to take the oil off the tables.

ASSESSMENT

Consider the following:
● Are the children able to cut out individual circles?
● Are the children able to hold the markers properly and decorate their globes?
● Are the children able to oil their sheets of paper?

Sue Bradford Edwards, Florissant, MO

Children's Books

Earth Day by
David F. Marx
The Lorax by Dr. Seuss
Miss Rumphius by
Barbara Cooney

Trashy Art

4+

Materials

recyclable materials
(juice boxes,
paper scraps,
empty paper
towel tubes, and
so on)
glue (craft and
sticks)
collage materials
(pompoms,
sequins, chenille
stems, plastic
glitter, and so on)

LEARNING OBJECTIVES

The children will:
1. Understand that recycling common objects keeps them from ending up in landfills.
2. Develop their imaginations as they turn common objects into works of art.

VOCABULARY

artwork	design	landfill	trash
collage	glue	recycle	
create	hole punch	scraps	

PREPARATION

- Ahead of time, set out a bin and ask the children to bring in recyclable materials.

WHAT TO DO

1. Set up an area where the children can create their Trashy Art. Set out the craft supplies and collage items (pompoms, sequins, chenille stems, plastic glitter, buttons, fabric scraps, and so on).
2. Closely supervise the children as they use their imaginations to create their own unique artwork out of the recyclable materials.
3. Encourage conversation by asking many open-ended questions and making positive comments on the children's work. For example, "I see that you are putting a lot of purple pompoms on the top your artwork. Is there a special reason for using that color?"
4. As the children work, talk with them about what would have happened to their recycled items if they had put those items in the trash. Introduce the idea of a landfill and briefly explain what that is.

ASSESSMENT

Consider the following:
- Gauge what the children have learned by asking them to continue collecting recyclable items and to sort recyclable items from nonrecyclable ones as a part of the daily routine.
- Can the children describe the artistic way they enjoy their recycled objects?

Children's Books

The Great Trash Bash by
Loreen Leedy
Painted Dreams by
Karen Lynn Williams
Recycle Every Day! by
Nancy Elizabeth Wallace
Trashy Town by
Andrea Zimmerman
and David Clemesha

Virginia Jean Herrod, Columbia, SC

Book Box Storage

5+

LEARNING OBJECTIVES

The children will:

1. Demonstrate small motor skills through the use of child-safe scissors, glue sticks, and markers.
2. Develop creativity while exploring the concept of recycling.

Materials

empty cereal boxes (1 per child and adult)
pencils
child-safe scissors
glue sticks
markers
scrap paper, such as extra worksheets

VOCABULARY

| dump | neat | recycle | store |
| garbage | organize | reuse | tidy |

PREPARATION

- Cut off the top of each cereal box, at a slight angle so the remaining box is shaped like a magazine organizer.

WHAT TO DO

1. Explain to the children that when we throw things away, they are taken to the garbage dump. We can cut down on garbage by recycling and reusing. The book box they make will also help organize their rooms, keeping their books neatly in one place.
2. Have the children trace the sides of their boxes on the paper. Assist as needed.
3. Have them cut out the paper and glue it onto the box, so that the clean side of the paper faces out. Assist as needed.
4. Ask the children to use markers to put their names and other decorations on their boxes. Now they can help keep their world and their room neat and tidy.

TEACHER-TO-TEACHER TIP

- This project can be scheduled to coincide with the school book fair.

ASSESSMENT

Consider the following:

- Can the child trace the box shape and cut the paper?
- Is the child able to correctly glue the paper onto the box?
- Is the child able to decorate the box?

Children's Books

The Lorax by Dr. Seuss
The Big Beautiful Brown Box by Larry Dane Brimner
But, Excuse Me, That Is My Book by Lauren Child
My Book Box by Will Hillenbrand

Sue Bradford Edwards, Florissant, MO

Earth Day T-Shirts

5+

LEARNING OBJECTIVES

The children will:
1. Develop their fine motor skills.
2. Learn to express themselves creatively while integrating earth science.

white T-shirt (1 per child)
old magazines or pieces of cardboard
medium-sized ball or round object (perhaps a round sponge)
green and blue fabric paint
green and blue permanent markers
alphabet stencils

VOCABULARY

Earth Day   recycle   T-shirt

WHAT TO DO

1. Give each child a T-shirt and let him place cardboard or newspaper inside to prevent markers from bleeding through.
2. Help each child dip the ball or sponge in blue paint and make a circle in the center of the shirt to form the Earth.
3. After the blue paint dries, encourage the children to use green paint to create land areas.
4. Finally, help the children stencil their names in green and blue permanent marker. You might even stencil something like "Happy Earth Day" or "Take Care of Our Earth" across the fronts of the shirts as well.

ASSESSMENT

Consider the following:
- Are the children able to manipulate the sponges and create Earth shapes at the centers of their shirts?
- Do the children express an understanding that the images of the Earth on their shirts are meant to stand for the Earth itself?
- Are the children able to stencil their names with ease?

Lisa Chichester, Parkersburg, WV

Children's Books

Earth Day by David F. Marx
The Lorax by Dr. Seuss
Why Should I Recycle? by Jen Green

Litter Bugs

5+

LEARNING OBJECTIVES

The children will:

1. Use small motor skills to make "bug bodies."
2. Develop their small motor skills by using tape and/or glue.

Materials

newspaper
tape
plastic utensils
plastic caps
wiggle eyes
glue

VOCABULARY

dispose	litter	recycling bin	trash
garbage	litter bug	streams	trash can

WHAT TO DO

1. Explain to the children that when we drop trash on the ground, we are "litter bugs." This trash can wash into streams and cause problems for animals, plants, and people. We need to make sure litter goes into trash cans and recycling bins.
2. Have each child wad up a piece of newspaper. They should make a ball about the size of a baseball. Use tape to keep it in a ball shape.
3. Have the children select plastic utensils for legs, a plastic cap for a hat, and wiggle eyes. They can then glue or tape these items onto their litter bugs.
4. Arrange these litter bugs around the room to remind everyone that litter goes in specific places.

ASSESSMENT

Consider the following:

- Can each child make a paper ball body?
- Can each child add limbs, a cap, and eyes to a paper ball body?

Sue Bradford Edwards, Florissant, MO

Children's Books

Smash, Mash, Crash! There Goes the Trash by Barbara Odanaka
The Tin Forest by Helen Ward and Wayne Anderson
Trashy Town by Andrea Zimmerman and David Clemesha

Recycling Cans

5+

LEARNING OBJECTIVES

The children will:
1. Learn that items can have many different uses.
2. Develop their small motor skills.

Materials

empty and clean
cans of any size
decorating
materials, such as
paper, paint and
brushes, stickers,
masking tape,
and discarded
wallpaper books
(many stores are
glad to give you
these books free
of charge)
soil
nail (adult use only)
seeds

VOCABULARY

can   plant   recycle   seed

WHAT TO DO

1. Encourage the children to tell you what a particular can was used for (coffee, soup, vegetables, and so on).
2. Have the children think of something else they can use the can for. There is of course the usual pencil, marker, or crayon holder, but then every so often a child has an entirely different idea, like a "bad dream catcher" to put on the night stand.
3. After the children have brainstormed a few ideas, set out the various decorating items and encourage the children to decorate their cans any way they like.
4. After the children finish decorating their cans, help them turn the cans into seed planters.
5. At the bottom of the can use the nail to make a hole so water may drain (adult-only step).
6. Help the children fill the cans with soil, and then plant either wild flower seeds or herb seeds in them.
7. Over time, remind the children to water their cans lightly and keep the soil moist.

TEACHER-TO-TEACHER TIP
- Parsley and chives work quite well for planting. Coffee can planters make great Mother's Day gifts.

ASSESSMENT
Consider the following:
- Do the children understand the idea that objects can have many uses?
- Do the children understand the importance of not being wasteful?

Ingelore Mix, Gainesville, VA

Children's Books

The Berenstain Bears Don't Pollute (Anymore) by Stan and Jan Berenstain
The Lorax by Dr. Seuss
Nate the Great Goes Down in the Dumps by Marjorie Weinman Sharmat

Eco Art: Rodia Replicas

5+

LEARNING OBJECTIVES

The children will:

1. Learn about a man named Simon Rodia, who created the amazing Watts Towers out of the scraps and junk he could find.
2. Build their own structures out of scrap materials.

Materials

prints of internet photos of the Watts Towers in Los Angeles mounted on poster board

cardboard sheets or boxes from cereal, crackers, and other food products

cardboard paper towel tubes

newspaper

child-safe scissors

decorating materials, such as glitter, scraps of foil, buttons, pebbles, beads, and bottle caps

VOCABULARY

cardboard	junk	sculpture	Simon Rodia	tube
cylinder	reuse	set	structure	Watts Towers

PREPARATION

- Collect cardboard pieces well in advance.
- Cut the cardboard boxes into flat sheets and place them in the art area for the project.

WHAT TO DO

1. Start in the block area. Show the poster to the children and explain that a poor construction worker named Simon Rodia built 17 structures, two of which stood almost 100 feet tall. He collected scraps and worked in his spare time for 33 years to create these wonderful Watts Towers.
2. Encourage the children to use blocks or manipulatives to make structures similar to those they see in the photos.
3. Later move to the art area. Cut slots halfway up the center of each cardboard piece and show the children how to join them together to stand up. Cut two slots at the bottom of the cardboard cylinders (tubes) so they can be added to the structures.
4. Once the structures have been formed, the children may paint and decorate them.
5. Put the structures on display in the block area. People may "visit" this special exhibition.

ASSESSMENT

Consider the following:

- Evaluate the constructive and creative skills used by the children.
- Do the children build their own towers?

Children's Books

It's Earth Day! by Mercer Mayer
Michael Recycle by Ellie Bethel
Trash and Recycling by Stephanie Turnbull

Susan Sharkey, Fletcher Hills, CA

Little Earths

3+

LEARNING OBJECTIVES

The children will:
1. Identify the colors green, blue, white, and brown.
2. Understand that when viewed from space the Earth looks like a multicolored ball or marble.

Materials

The Earth and I by
Frank Asch
photo of Earth
white paper plates
sponges (four for
each child—
triangular
cosmetic sponges
work great)
small flat containers
for paint
green, blue, white,
and brown
fingerpaint
paper towels

VOCABULARY

blue	color	palette	sponge
brown	Earth	pattern	view
cloud	green	space	white

WHAT TO DO

1. Read *The Earth and I* by Frank Asch with the children. As you read, help the children notice the color patterns on each page.
2. After reading, show the children the photo of the Earth as viewed from space. Point out the colors green, brown, blue, and white.
3. Give each child a paper plate, four sponges, and four small pans of green, blue, white, and brown paint.
4. Show the children how to use the sponges to paint the three colors on the Earth shape. As the children mix the colors on the paper, it will resemble Earth as viewed from space.
5. Show the children how to crumple up a paper towel and blot the painting to remove the extra paint. The blotting also creates a pattern in the paint that will make it resemble the Earth even more. Then, the children can paint white clouds over the Earth.
6. Let the paintings dry. Display them on a bulletin board with a title appropriate for your theme.

Children's Books

Big Earth, Little Me by
Thom Wiley
*Blast Off to Earth! A
Look at Geography* by
Loreen Leedy
*The Librarian Who
Measured the Earth* by
Kathryn Lasky and
Kevin Hawkes

ASSESSMENT

Consider the following:
- Do any of the children have trouble grasping the sponges or getting the paint where they want it?
- As the children work, ask them to identify the colors on their paintings.

Virginia Jean Herrod, Columbia, SC

Trash to Treasure

3+

LEARNING OBJECTIVES

The children will:

1. Reuse recyclable materials (trash) to create works of art (treasures).
2. Practice creative thinking and problem-solving skills.

Materials

box
recyclable materials
   (see list to the
   right)
standard art
   supplies
   (markers, paint,
   glue, tape,
   string/yarn,
   child-safe
   scissors, hole
   punches, and
   so on)

VOCABULARY

create   recycle   reuse   trash   treasure

PREPARATION

- Set up a large collection box near your parent/family member area in advance. Post a notice as follows:
  Let's get ready for Trash-to-Treasure Day! Please donate plastic lids, egg cartons, cardboard boxes, magazines, colorful junk mail, cylinders from paper towels, foam trays, berry baskets, paper bags, gift wrap, and so on.
- Move the collection box to the art area.

WHAT TO DO

1. Read and discuss one or more of the related books (see list for suggestions). Explain that you will help the children turn trash into treasure by reusing materials in fun new ways.
2. Invite small groups to the art area and encourage them to examine the "trash." Ask them to think about what "treasures" they might create using this and other art supplies.
3. Demonstrate a few techniques to get the ball rolling. For example, cut a magazine picture into a circle and glue it to a margarine lid. Send it through the air like a flying disc or punch a hole at the edge and tie a piece of yarn to spin it overhead.
4. Provide inspiration and encouragement. Assist the children as needed.

Children's Books

*I Can Save the Earth!
One Little Monster
Learns to Reduce,
Reuse, and Recycle* by
Alison Inches
Reusing and Recycling
by Charlotte Guillain
Trash and Recycling by
Stephanie Turnbull

ASSESSMENT

Consider the following:

- Invite the children to show off their treasures and explain how they made them.
- Do the children understand the value of reusing old items?

Susan Sharkey, Fletcher Hills, CA

The Adventures of a Plastic Bottle

4+

LEARNING OBJECTIVES

The children will:
1. Learn why we should recycle.
2. Learn how bottles are made.
3. Learn how fleece is made from a plastic bottle.

Materials

The Adventures of a Plastic Bottle: A Story About Recycling by Alison Inches
fleece jacket
plastic bottle

VOCABULARY

diary	garbage	manufacturing
fleece	landfill	recycling

WHAT TO DO

1. Read to the children *The Adventures of a Plastic Bottle: A Story About Recycling* by Alison Inches. This will show them recycling from a new perspective. It is the diary of a plastic bottle as it goes on a journey from the refinery plant to the manufacturing line to the store shelf to a garbage can and finally to a recycling plant where it emerges into its new life as a fleece jacket! The diary entries are fun, but point out the ecological significance behind each product and the resources used to make it.
2. Discuss the book with the children and talk about landfills and why we should recycle.
3. Have a fleece jacket available so the children can compare how soft it is compared to a plastic bottle.

TEACHER-TO-TEACHER TIP
• Recycle and make other things from plastic bottles.

SONG
Sing "Ten Green Bottles Hanging on the Wall" with the children.

ASSESSMENT
Consider the following:
• Ask the children what can be made from plastic bottles.
• Can the children tell you why we should recycle?
• Do the children know what a landfill is?

Children's Books

Recycle! A Handbook for Kids by Gail Gibbons
Where Does the Garbage Go? by Paul Showers
Why Should I Recycle? by Jen Green

Anne Adeney, Plymouth, United Kingdom

Cactus

4+

LEARNING OBJECTIVES

The children will:
1. Learn to engage their curiosity.
2. Develop observation skills.
3. Learn about protecting and caring for cacti.
4. Build a foundation for later learning in botany.

Materials

pictures of various cacti as well as pictures of other plants, such as roses, daffodils, vegetables, and more
drawing of a cactus on art paper (1 per child)
paper
colored pencils or crayons

VOCABULARY

botany   desert   saguaro cactus
cactus   plant   spine

PREPARATION

● If you or a parent has a potted cactus, bring it into the classroom. Be careful that the children don't touch it.

WHAT TO DO

1. Read one or more books about cacti. Do the children know where these plants grow? If you are in a desert area, they will have a better understanding.
2. If you live in another area, explain about deserts. Talk about how desert plants conserve water. Talk about how we can protect cacti by not taking them from the desert. How are desert plants different from other plants?
3. Show the children the pictures in the books as you read them.
4. Encourage the children to talk about any experiences with cacti.
5. Have the children color the cactus picture.
6. Be sure the children understand they should never touch a cactus—the spines can hurt!

ASSESSMENT

Consider the following:
● When shown pictures of various cacti and other plants, can the children tell you which are cacti?
● What can the children tell you about cacti?
● Do the children have ideas for how to protect these plants?

Shirley Anne Ramaley, Sun City, AZ

Children's Books

Cactus Café: A Story of the Sonoran Desert by Kathleen Weidner Zoehfeld
Cactus Desert by Donald M. Silver
Desert Giant: The World of the Saguaro Cactus by Barbara Bash
Saguaro Cactus by Paul Berquist

Crush a Can Each Day

4+

LEARNING OBJECTIVES

The children will:

1. Improve their awareness of aluminum recycling.
2. Develop their oral language and social skills.
3. Learn to follow directions.

Materials

aluminum beverage
   cans, rinsed and
   dried
carpet square
recycling bin or bag
5 sheets of colored
   copy paper

VOCABULARY

aluminum	commitment	foot
can	crush	recycle

PREPARATION

- List five children's names on each colored sheet of paper. Title each paper with one day of the week.
- Each morning display five aluminum cans on a table or shelf.
- Set the carpet square on the floor and the recycling bin nearby.

WHAT TO DO

1. Read one of the book selections listed below. With the children, discuss the importance of recycling aluminum.
2. Ask the children if they ever drank from an aluminum can. Ask, "What do you do with the can when you are done?" Allow time for the children to respond.
3. Invite five assigned children to stand in a line at front of the room.
4. Select a single child and teach the children the following chant and response:

   Child: *Good morning, friends.*
   Class: *Good morning, _____.* (class responds and fills in the child's name)
   Child: *Today, I'm going to recycle aluminum.* (child sets can on the carpet
      square, steps on the can and crushes it, then places it in the recycle bin)
   Class: *Thank you for taking care of our Earth!*

5. Repeat the chant until all five children crush a can.
6. Continue with five new children each day as your young learners learn the value and "fun" of recycling aluminum.

ASSESSMENT

Consider the following:

- Do the children appreciate the need to recycle aluminum cans?
- Are the children able to take turns saying the chant and following directions?

Children's Books

Follow That Trash! All About Recycling by Francine Jacobs
Recycle: A Handbook for Kids by Gail Gibbons
Reuse, Reduce, Recycle by Nuria Roca

Mary J. Murray, Mazomanie, WI

Recycle Even My Tricycle

LEARNING OBJECTIVES

The children will:

1. Understand that it is important to take care of the Earth every day.
2. Sort items into categories for recycling and reusing.
3. Understand and use vocabulary words associated with recycling, reusing, and reducing waste for keeping the Earth clean.

Materials

2 containers or garbage pails
5 objects each child brings from home
related children's books (see list for suggestions)
large sheets of paper folded into 3 sections (1 sheet per child)
crayons

VOCABULARY

aluminum	Earth	plastic
cardboard	exchange	sort
container	garbage	trade
donate	landfill	waste

PREPARATION

- Prepare containers by labeling them "recycle" and "reuse."
- Write a letter to families explaining the recycle, reuse, and reduce topic. In the letter, ask the families to reinforce recycling and sorting at home and to send things in to the classroom for this project.

WHAT TO DO

1. Read a book introducing the topic (see list for suggestions). Discuss the containers you labeled.
2. Collect items and help the children sort them into the containers.
3. Have a Reuse Books Day. Have the children bring in a book to exchange with their classmates.
4. Involve parents by having a Reuse Clothing Day for children to exchange clothing. Ask parents and family members to bring outgrown clothing sorted by size and set them out on a table in the school.

ASSESSMENT

Consider the following:

- Ask the children to draw pictures in the segmented paper to show they understand what recycle, reuse, and reduce mean.
- How well do the children sort the materials into different containers?

Carol Levy, Woodbury, NY

Children's Books

The Berenstain Bears Don't Pollute (Anymore) by Stan and Jan Berenstain
The Lorax by Dr. Seuss
Nate the Great Goes Down in the Dumps by Marjorie Weinman Sharmat
Recycle: A Handbook for Kids by Gail Gibbons
Reuse, Reduce, Recycle by Nuria Roca
Why Should I Recycle? by Jen Green

Block Compost

5+

LEARNING OBJECTIVES

The children will:
1. Learn about the value of compost.
2. Develop their small motor skills.

Materials

book about
  composting
colored blocks
barrel

VOCABULARY

compost	healthy	reuse
garden	recycle	vegetable

WHAT TO DO

1. Read a book about composting with the children (see listed for suggestions).
2. Engage the children in a discussion about composting.
3. Try to recreate a compost pile with blocks and a barrel (the compost).
4. Assign colored blocks for what would go in a compost heap, such as white for egg shells, blue for potato peels, orange for fall leaves, and green for grass clippings.
5. Talk about how the compost heap should be turned while the children turn over blocks inside the barrel.

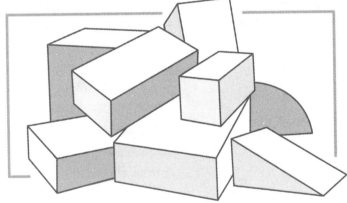

6. Scoop blocks inside the barrel out onto a pretend garden plot. Talk about how the compost will make the vegetables grow big and healthy.

ASSESSMENT

Consider the following:
● Do the children understand what composting involves?
● Do the children turn the compost pile?

Christine Kohler, Ballinger, TX

Children's Books

The Carrot Seed by Ruth Kraus
The Everything Kids' Environment Book by Sheri Amsel
Growing Vegetable Soup by Lois Ehlert
The Surprise Garden by Zoe Hall
What's Going on in the Compost Pile? by Rachel Chappell

Earth Day Awareness

5+

LEARNING OBJECTIVES

The children will:
1. Name ways they can care for the Earth.
2. Learn about pollution.

Materials

chart paper
markers
flowers from a
    garden
The Earth and I by
    Frank Asch
plastic bags (1 per
    child)
pieces of trash

VOCABULARY

bottles	flowers	messy	pretty	sod
cans	littering	pollution	recycle	trash

PREPARATION

- Draw a line down the middle of the chart paper. On the left side draw a happy Earth. On the right side draw a sad-faced Earth.

WHAT TO DO

1. Show the children the flowers. Explain that flowers make the Earth pretty. Ask the children what else they see outside. Some things are pretty, but some things are messy. Explain that you are going to read about a boy who wanted to make the Earth pretty.
2. Read *The Earth and I* by Frank Asch. Ask the children questions about the book. What did the boy do to help the Earth? Record the children's responses on the left side of the chart paper. What made the boy sad? Record the children's responses on the right side of the paper.
3. Discuss pollution and littering. Drop some trash onto the floor. Does that look pretty or messy? Tell them that littering and pollution make the Earth very sad. Give each child or pair of children a plastic bag in which to pick up trash. Tell them you can recycle any cans and bottles.
4. Go into your school yard and pick up litter. Discuss your findings.

TEACHER-TO-TEACHER TIP

- Supervise the children closely as they pick up trash outside. If they see anything they don't recognize, they should tell you so they don't get hurt.

ASSESSMENT

Consider the following:
- Return to the chart after the activity. Ask the children if there is anything else they could add that makes the Earth happy or sad. What can they do at home?
- Do the children understand the meaning of the word "recycle"?

Children's Books

For the Love of Our Earth by P. K. Hallinan
Reduce and Reuse by Salley Hewitt
Why Should I Recycle Garbage? by M. J. Knight

Tina Cho, La Habra, CA

Earth Day Pledge

5+

LEARNING OBJECTIVES

The children will:
1. Identify three or more ways children can help care for the Earth.
2. Understand the importance of caring for the Earth.

Materials

It's Earth Day! by
   Mercer Mayer
poster board
marker
green washable
   paint
paint pan
paper towels

VOCABULARY

air	conservation	handprint	recycle	worth
clean	fresh	home	sun	

PREPARATION
● Print "Earth-Day Pledge" on poster board.

WHAT TO DO
1. On Earth Day or any other day, read *It's Earth Day!* by Mercer Mayer to the children. Pause occasionally throughout the book to discuss different ideas with the children.
2. Continue discussing with the children ways to care for the Earth. Ask the children if the story gave them any ideas about new ways to care for the Earth.
3. Set out the poster board with the following pledge, along with the paint, paint pan, and paper towels.

   Earth-Day Pledge by Kathryn Hake
   Our handprints show how much we care.
   We want clean water and fresh air.
   So we will help protect the Earth,
   Showing others its great worth.

4. Pour a small amount of the paint into the paint pan, and invite the children to take turns putting their handprints on the poster. **Note:** Be sure to observe carefully, and have the children wash their hands immediately after making their handprints.
5. When the paint dries, set the pledge poster on the wall as a reminder to the children.

ASSESSMENT
Consider the following:
● Do the children have an understanding of what Earth Day is, and why it is important?
● Do the children understand the importance of the pledge?

Kathryn Hake, Brownsville, OR

Children's Books

Earth Day Birthday by
Pattie Schnetzler
The Earth and I by
Frank Asch
Why Should I Recycle?
by Jen Green

The Earth, Our Home

5+

LEARNING OBJECTIVES

The children will:
1. Describe various environments on Earth.
2. Explain two or more ways to help care for the Earth.

Materials

globe
People and the Environment by Jennifer Boothroyd
crayons
large sheets of construction paper cut into circles
magazines, catalogs, and newspapers containing outdoor images
glue

VOCABULARY

beach	forest	mountain	valley
desert	globe	nature	stream
Earth	island	ocean	
environment	lake	river	

WHAT TO DO

1. Gather the children in a circle.
2. Explain that today you are going to talk about the Earth. Show the children a globe.
3. Talk with the children about the globe, how this is a model of where we live. Point out how much of the Earth is covered with water. There are oceans, lakes, rivers, and streams. The rest of the Earth is land: mountains, valleys, deserts, beaches, and islands. The Earth is a special place for us to live. Tell the children that we need to help take care of it because it is our home.
4. Read *People and the Environment* by Jennifer Boothroyd, pausing as necessary to discuss and answer questions the children have about our home and its environment, the land and nature around us here on Earth.
5. Set out the various collage materials.
6. Invite the children to tear images from the magazines and catalogs and to make collages on the circular construction paper. Talk with the children about their collages as they work.

ASSESSMENT

Consider the following:
- Ask the children what they can do to help care for the Earth.
- Do the children understand the importance of caring for the Earth?

Children's Books

The Earth and I by Frank Asch
For the Love of Our Earth by P. K. Hallinan
Our Earth: Making Less Trash by Peggy Hock

Kathryn Hake, Brownsville, OR

Lakes and Ponds

5+

LEARNING OBJECTIVES

The children will:
1. Learn about lakes and ponds.
2. Learn about safety.
3. Develop their writing skills.

Materials

large board
pencils
writing paper

VOCABULARY

animals	boat	lake	pond	water
bird	fish	plants	swim	

PREPARATION

- Write the letters on a large board for all the children to see.

WHAT TO DO

1. Read one or more of the books about lakes and ponds (see list for suggestions). Ask the children what they know about lakes or ponds. Discuss the importance of safety and of staying with an adult at a lake or pond.

2. Talk with the children, explaining some of the following points about lakes and ponds:

   - Animals and plants live together in lakes and ponds.
   - We should never throw trash or garbage into the water.
   - We always leave the animals and birds alone.
   - We don't pick the plants.
   - Lakes are bigger than ponds.
   - Lakes are too large to support plant growth at the bottom, while ponds have plants growing throughout.
   - People like to fish, swim, and boat on lakes.

3. Write "lake" and "pond" on the board. Have the children practice writing the letters for "lake" and "pond" and signing their names. Some of the children might want to list more words related to lakes and ponds. If so, add those to the board.

ASSESSMENT

Consider the following:
- Can the children tell you the difference between a lake and a pond?
- Do the children know what to do when they see a bird or animal? Ask them about the plants. What do people like to do at lakes?

Children's Books

Lake and Pond by April Pulley Sayre
Lake and Pond: Food Webs by Paul Fleisher
Lakes, Ponds, and Temporary Pools by David Josephs

Shirley Anne Ramaley, Sun City, AZ

Reuse It Day!

5+

LEARNING OBJECTIVES

The children will:

1. Learn a fundamental lesson about recycling and reusing found objects.
2. Make a practical object from recycled material.
3. Learn how to reuse a found object.

Materials

empty boxes or
  cardboard
  containers
newspaper
markers or paints
  suitable for
  cardboard
paintbrushes
child-safe scissors
construction paper
glue
paint smocks
  (optional)

VOCABULARY

| box | label | recycle | reuse |
| decorate | pencil holder | reduce | storage container |

PREPARATION

- Prior to the day on which you do this activity, ask the children to bring in clean empty boxes or containers.
- Cover tables with newspaper.

WHAT TO DO

1. Read several books on recycling and reusing materials.
2. Teach the children the phrase "reduce, reuse, recycle."
3. Share some stories about how people in the past have reused objects instead of buying them.
4. Have the children make either a pencil holder or storage container from their empty box.
5. Let the children decorate their boxes with markers or paint.
6. Cut out label from construction paper. Decorate.
7. Write "Pencils" (or another word if the box is used for something else) on label.
8. Glue the label to the box. Painted boxes will need to dry first.

TEACHER-TO-TEACHER TIP

- Protect surfaces with newspapers if the children are going to paint their boxes.

ASSESSMENT

Consider the following:

- Do the children learn how to reuse a found object?
- Can the children see possibilities in recycling other found objects?
- Do the children learn to reuse instead of throwing things away?
- Are the children more aware of how reusing objects helps to save our natural resources?

Children's Books

Our Earth: Making Less Trash by Peggy Hock
Reduce and Reuse by Salley Hewitt
Reusing Things by Susan Barraclough
Why Should I Recycle Garbage? by M. J. Knight

Donna Alice Patton, Hillsboro, OH

Rivers and Streams

5+

LEARNING OBJECTIVES

The children will:

1. Develop curiosity about rivers, streams, and the environment.
2. Learn respect for the environment.
3. Learn the importance of rivers and streams.
4. Develop a foundation for later learning in the sciences and nature.

Materials

VOCABULARY

animals	environment	habitat	protect	water
birds	fact	lake	river	wildlife
ecology	freshwater	ocean	stream	

WHAT TO DO

1. Sit in a circle. Read one of the books from the list below or one similar.
2. Share these facts with the children and encourage discussion:
   - All rivers and streams start at a high point, like a mountain or a hill.
   - Most of these are freshwater. (Explain this to the children.)
   - Rivers are bigger than streams.
   - Water from a spring or snow melt starts at a high point and flows downhill.
   - Other small streams combine to form bigger streams and eventually a river.
   - Water then flows into the ocean or a lake.
3. Ask the children if they know why rivers and streams are important. Some ideas:
   - They provide habitat for animals and birds.
   - They are waterways for shipping and businesses.
   - We enjoy their beauty.
   - Families have fun together boating and fishing.
4. Ask the children about how they help protect rivers and streams. Some ideas include:
   - Don't throw trash or waste into the water.
   - Watch the animals and birds but don't disturb them.
   - Observe boating rules.

ASSESSMENT

Consider the following:

- Ask the children to describe a river and a stream.
- Can the children describe how rivers and streams form?
- Do the children have ideas on how we can protect rivers and streams?

Children's Books

Living Near a River by Allan Fowler
Rivers and Streams by Jenny Vaughan and Angela Royston
What Lives in Streams and Rivers? by Oona Gaarder-Juntti

Shirley Anne Ramaley, Sun City, AZ

Saving Our Planet

5+

LEARNING OBJECTIVES

The children will:
1. Describe some of the problems of our planet Earth.
2. Increase their awareness of the responsibility they share in protecting our planet.

Materials

The Lorax by
    Dr. Seuss
digital camera (if
    available)
*Sammy & Sue Go
    Green Too* by
    Suzanne Corso
drawing paper
markers

VOCABULARY

beautiful	litter	planet	reduce
environment	neighborhood	pollution	responsibility
identify	observe	recycle	reuse

What to Do

1. Read *The Lorax* by Dr. Seuss to the children. Allow the children to respond to the information presented in the story and share observations they have made about problems in their environment.
2. Take the children on a "pollution safari" in the neighborhood and help them identify local issues. If you have a digital camera, use it to record the problems the children identify as they walk. Use these photos to help the children remember what they saw on the walk, and for strengthening literacy skills if combined with related vocabulary/print such as in an experience chart.
3. Read *Sammy & Sue Go Green Too* by Suzanne Corso. Talk about the story. Discuss the issues and help the children relate them to their own lives.
4. Ask each child to choose one way she can help make our Earth a more beautiful place. Then ask each child to draw a picture and write a statement at the bottom of the picture (or take dictation from the child and record it for them).
5. Photocopy the pictures and guide the children to collate and staple the class pictures together to create a "Save Our Planet Earth" book to share with their families or other classes.

ASSESSMENT

Consider the following:
- Can the children identify problems on the pollution safari?
- Do the children's illustrations indicate an understanding of how to care for the Earth?

Children's Books

The Dumpster Diver by
    Janet S. Wong
Smiling Planet by
    Deane Freddy
*Stuff: Reduce, Reuse,
Recycle* by Steven Kroll

Patricia Enright, Jersey City, NJ

Traveling to Save the Earth 5+

LEARNING OBJECTIVES

The children will:
1. Learn about environmentally friendly ways to travel.
2. Learn about cooperation.
3. Develop their large motor skills.
4. Develop their social skills.

Materials

book on transportation
whistle

VOCABULARY

bike	exhaust	pollution	scooter	travel
boat	gas	ride	skateboard	wagon
driver	motor	rollerblades	transportation	walk

WHAT TO DO

1. Read the children a book about travel (see list for suggestions).
2. After reading the book, engage the children in a discussion about the effects of travel. Explain that certain forms of transportation generate exhaust, which is a kind of pollution.
3. Invite the children to stand up and pretend to use different modes of transportation that do not require the use of motors or other things that will harm the environment. For example, you may say, "Everyone ride their bikes." All the children pretend to get on their bikes and ride around the yard.
4. After a few minutes, blow the whistle so the children will stop.
5. Name another mode of transportation for the children to act out.

TEACHER-TO-TEACHER TIP

- Ask the children to suggest ideas for different travel modes and use those in the game.

Children's Books

For the Love of Our Earth by P. K. Hallinan
On the Go by Ann Morris
Transportation by Margaret C. Hall

ASSESSMENT

Consider the following:
- How well do the children pretend to use the various named modes of transportation?
- Are the children able to begin to understand the importance of reducing air pollution?

Eileen Lucas, Fort McMurray, Alberta, Canada

Windmills

5+

Materials

chalk
chalkboard or
  poster board
paper
pencils, crayons, or
  markers
pictures of
  windmills

LEARNING OBJECTIVES

The children will:
1. Develop language skills.
2. Learn about windmills.
3. Learn about wind power and how it helps the Earth.
4. Develop beginning reading skills.

VOCABULARY

electricity	environment	wind power
energy	Holland	windmill

PREPARATION
- Write the vocabulary words in chalk on a board or in large writing on a poster.
- Place pictures of windmills where the children can see them.

WHAT TO DO
1. Read the children one of the books listed here. Talk with the children about windmills. Has anyone seen a windmill? Do the children know why windmills are used? Have they heard about windmills in Holland? What about in the United States?
2. Discuss the vocabulary words. Ask the children if they can tell you what the words mean. For words they don't know, explain the meaning. Talk about the importance of windmills in the future.
3. At the tables, have the children draw a windmill and add any vocabulary words on the papers below the picture of the windmill. Have them sign their names.

ASSESSMENT
Consider the following:
- Can the children tell you the meaning of the vocabulary words?
- What can they tell you about windmills?

Shirley Anne Ramaley, Sun City, AZ

Children's Books

Don't Go Up a Windmill: Poems by Steve Rideout
Generating Wind Power by Niki Walker
Mandie and the Windmill's Message by Lois Gladys Leppard
The Wind at Work: An Activity Guide to Windmills by Gretchen Woelfle

Trash, Trash Everywhere **3+**

LEARNING OBJECTIVES

The children will:
1. Learn why they shouldn't litter.
2. Learn how they can help to keep the Earth clean.
3. Learn where they should put trash.

Materials

junk mail and other
   paper waste
recycling bins

VOCABULARY

garbage   litter   messy   recycling   trash

PREPARATION

● Before the children arrive, crumple up junk mail or other paper and spread it around the classroom. The messier it looks the better.

WHAT TO DO

1. Give the children a few minutes to take in the mess.
2. Ask the children to join you for circle time.
3. Ask them how they think the room looks. You should get lots of comments about how messy it is.
4. Explain that when people don't put their trash in garbage cans where it belongs, it makes a big mess.
5. Ask the children to help you clean up the classroom and recycle the paper. Set out recycling bins into which the children can put all the paper.
6. Once the mess is gone, ask the children how they think the room looks now. Reinforce the fact that throwing trash on the ground makes the world look messy and can be harmful to the Earth.

ASSESSMENT

Consider the following:
● Take the children on a walk, and have them pick up real-life litter.
● Ask the children to draw a picture of what the world would look like if everyone littered.

Erin Huffstetler, Maryville, TN

Children's Books

I Stink! by
Kate McMullan
*Smash! Mash! Crash!
There Goes the Trash* by
Barbara Odanaka
Trashy Town by
Andrea Zimmerman
and David Clemesha

Flower Gazing

LEARNING OBJECTIVES

The children will:
1. Develop a greater appreciation of flowers.
2. Practice sharing and patience.

Materials

variety of garden and store-bought flowers (common dandelions would work as well as long-stemmed roses)
white board or poster

VOCABULARY

beautiful	feel	petals	stem
color words	flower	smell	touch
describe	leaves	stamen	

WHAT TO DO

1. Show the children the bouquet and ask what colors and shapes they see. Where can we find flowers? Does anyone have flowers at home? Why are there so many different kinds of beautiful flowers?
2. Choose an attractive flower such as a lily and have the children describe its appearance. Write these words on a white board or poster. Point out features such as the stem, leaves, petals, and stamen. Add these to your written list.
3. Next, hand the flower to the first child in the circle and invite her to examine it closely, to smell, touch, and even "listen to" it. Explain that when she hears the bell (or some other kind of signal you give) she will pass the flower to the next child in the circle.
4. Allow each child to hold and look at the flower. After it has gone around the circle, distribute the rest of the flowers so that each child has one in hand. Invite the children to gaze at their flowers in silence until they hear the bell. Now ask them to share their comments. What does your flower smell like? How does it feel to touch it? What color is your flower?

TEACHER-TO-TEACHER TIP

● You could also break the circle into groups of two, three, or four children and have these smaller groups share a single flower.

ASSESSMENT

Consider the following:
● Can the children accurately describe the flowers?
● Can the children name the various parts of the flowers?

Children's Books

Abuelito's Greenhouse by Susan Ring
Mr. Percy's Magic Greenhouse by Anthea Kemp
Out and About at the Greenhouse by Bitsy Kemper

Patrick Mitchell, Yagoto, Nagoya, Japan

Help the Earth

4+

LEARNING OBJECTIVES

The children will:
1. Learn various ways to care for the Earth.
2. Learn about the importance of caring for the Earth.

Materials

clean, empty soup cans
colored paper
buttons
stickers
beads
tree seedling
newspaper
glue
glossy magazines
child-safe scissors
colored felt
pencils

VOCABULARY

compost	Earth Day	insects	plant	reduce	seedling
decorate	garden	necklace	recycle	reuse	thread

WHAT TO DO

1. On Earth Day (April 22) or on any day, talk to the children about how they can help the environment by practicing the three "Rs": reduce, reuse, and recycle.
2. Following is a list of possible activities to do with the children. Choose one to do and decide when you will do the others.
   - Start a compost pile for lunch leftovers and yard waste.
   - Reuse clean soup cans to make pencil holders. Have the children cover a can with paper or fabric and decorate with buttons, stickers, or beads.
   - Plant a tree seedling, if possible. Give it lots of space.
   - Use old newspaper and glue to make papier-mâché gifts (vase, box, or ornament).
   - Ask parents and family members to reuse their plastic bags from the supermarket for the month.
   - Encourage the children's families to pack garbage-free lunches.
   - Plant a garden or window box to attract helpful insects.
   - Use both sides of sheets of paper for a whole day.
   - Make bead necklaces from old glossy magazines. Cut colorful pages into different-sized triangles. Roll the triangles tightly around a pencil one at a time, wide side first. Put glue on the last corner and hold it tight until dry. Pull the "bead" from the pencil. Make enough beads to make a necklace. Thread beads onto a piece of wool and tie the ends together.

Children's Books

Garbage and Recycling by Helen Orme
Our Earth: Making Less Trash by Peggy Hock
Reusing Things by Susan Barraclough

ASSESSMENT

Consider the following:
- Which activities do the children find most engaging? What do the children enjoy most about those activities?
- Do the children understand the importance of caring for the Earth?

Amelia Griffin, Ontario, Canada

It Starts with a Seed

4+

LEARNING OBJECTIVES

The children will:
1. Learn that big trees come from tiny seeds.
2. Learn that even small actions (such as planting a seed) can have a big impact.

Materials

different tree seeds (acorns, sweet gum pods, walnuts, maple "helicopter" seeds, cherries, pinecones, and so on)
drawing paper
crayons
pictures of the mature trees from the seeds you selected

Note: Deforestation has had a big impact on our planet: habitat loss, soil erosion, and decreased rainfall to name a few. By planting new trees, we help care for our planet. In this activity, children will begin to understand the long journey a tree makes from seed to mature plant and the importance of the end result.

VOCABULARY

grow	mature	planting	seed	tiny	tree

WHAT TO DO

1. Hand out a different seed to each child but do not explain to them what kind of tree it comes from.
2. Ask the children to use their imaginations to draw a picture of what the tree will look like once it grows to maturity. Have them draw themselves next to the tree for scale purposes.
3. When they finish, show the children the pictures of the mature trees. Ask them questions about their drawings. Are the drawings similar to the real tree? Are the mature trees as big as they thought they would be? How can something so large come from something so tiny? Have they ever planted a tree?
4. When finished, invite the children to take the seeds home to plant them.

TEACHER-TO-TEACHER TIP

- When assigning materials to children younger than four, make sure to stick with edible offerings (such as cherries and walnuts). When handing out nuts, please keep allergies in mind.

ASSESSMENT

Consider the following:
- Do the children understand that trees grow from small seeds?
- Can the children describe the shapes of the different seeds?

Children's Books

Abuelito's Greenhouse by Susan Ring
The Lorax by Dr. Seuss
Mr. Percy's Magic Greenhouse by Anthea Kemp
Trees by David Burnie

Monica Shaughnessy, Katy, TX

Michael Recycle

LEARNING OBJECTIVES

The children will:
1. Improve their oral language skills.
2. Begin to understand the concept of recycling.

Materials

puppet
materials for
   recycling
recycling bin
2' × 3' piece of
   cardboard
marker

VOCABULARY

aluminum	paper	recycle	sing
glass	plastic	save	thank you

PREPARATION

- Select a puppet to become your class recycling mascot. Name it Michael Recycle. Display the puppet in a prominent place to be used on a regular basis during your circle or group time activities.
- Display a bin of recyclable materials near the puppet.
- Print "Michael Recycle" in large bold letters on the sheet of cardboard. This will be your puppet stage.

WHAT TO DO

1. Each morning before the children come to the circle time area, set out the recyclable materials in a large circle formation on the floor.
2. As children come to the circle area, have each child sit near a recyclable item.
3. Place the Michael Recycle puppet on your hand and manipulate the puppet behind the prepared puppet stage.
4. Display the recycling bin right below Michael and the cardboard stage.
5. Have Michael Recycle explain to the children the importance of recycling. Michael Recycle can ask the children what they are holding, and whether the items are recyclable.
6. Invite the children to take turns bringing up their recyclable items and putting them in the recycling bin. As they do so, Michael Recycle congratulates the children.
7. Encourage the children to congratulate one another after they each finish taking their turn recycling.

ASSESSMENT

Consider the following:
- Do the children understand the importance of recycling?
- Can the children differentiate between recyclable and nonrecyclable materials?

Children's Books

Michael Recycle by
Ellie Bethel
*Reducing and Recycling
Waste* by Carol Inskipp
Why Should I Recycle?
by Jen Green

Mary J. Murray, Mazomanie, WI

Recyclables Gobbling Machine

4+

LEARNING OBJECTIVES

The children will:

1. Learn to care for the environment.
2. Develop their fine motor skills and creative expression.
3. Learn about the importance of recycling.

Materials

cardboard boxes or
   giant papier-
   mâché animals
paint
paintbrushes
cotton balls
sequins
yarn
other decorative
   materials
pictures of
   recyclable and
   nonrecyclable
   items, laminated

VOCABULARY

environment	machine	reduce
gobbling	recycle	reuse

PREPARATION

● Set out boxes that the children can paint and decorate.

WHAT TO DO

1. Give each child a box, and encourage the children to paint and decorate them to look like gobbling machines.
2. Set out small laminated images of objects that are and are not recyclable.
3. Engage the children in a discussion about recycling, and explain how some objects are recyclable while others are not.
4. Challenge the children to "gobble" only the images of the objects that are recyclable. Encourage the children to talk to one another about which objects they think are and are not recyclable.

   Note: The children love this game and there is lots of discussion and thinking that goes on throughout the game.

POEM

My Gobbling Machine by Eileen Lucas
My gobbling machine goes munch, munch, munch.
It makes a funny sound.
It takes my recyclables everyday
So I don't have to throw them away.

ASSESSMENT

Consider the following:

● Do the children understand the difference between what is recyclable and what isn't?
● Do you notice discussions about recycling going on?

Children's Books

Earth Mother by
   Ellen Jackson
*Mother Nature Nursery
   Rhymes* by
   Sandy Stryker,
Mindy Bingham, and
   Itoko Maeno
*Our Big Home
(An Earth Poem)* by
   Linda Glaser

Eileen Lucas, Fort McMurray, Alberta, Canada

Recycling

5+

2 large buckets
plastic bottles and
    dishes
paper towels
plastic or metal utensils
used containers (make
    sure these are safe
    with no rough edges)
other items, some of
    which can be
    recycled and others
    not

Children's Books

*I Can Save the Earth!
One Little Monster
Learns to Reduce,
Reuse, and Recycle* by
    Alison Inches
Michael Recycle by
    Ellie Bethel
*Michael Recycle Meets
Litterbug Doug* by
    Ellie Bethel
*Recycle! A Handbook
for Kids* by
    Gail Gibbons
*Where Does the
Garbage Go? Revised
Edition* by Paul Showers
Why Should I Recycle?
    by Jen Green

LEARNING OBJECTIVES

The children will:
1. Learn about recycling and why it helps our planet.
2. Learn what is recycled, if anything, in your area and how to do this.
3. Learn about landfills.

VOCABULARY

choice	landfill	trash
garbage	recycle	

PREPARATION
- Label the two buckets, one with "Recycle" and the other with "Garbage."
- Set out the materials in the dramatic play area.

WHAT TO DO
1. Sit together and discuss recycling, landfills, what happens to things we throw away, and choices to make with garbage and trash. Ask the children for their ideas.
2. Have each child pretend that she is taking out the trash.
3. Ask a child to put an item in the recycle or garbage container. Have the child explain her choice.
4. If the child doesn't have the right answer, carefully explain the proper choice.

ASSESSMENT
Consider the following:
- Ask the children to tell you about items that can be recycled.
- Can the children tell you what happens to those items?
- Do the children understand what happens to nonrecyclable items?

Shirley Anne Ramaley, Sun City, AZ

Toss It In!

LEARNING OBJECTIVES

The children will:
1. Identify basic recyclable materials.
2. Develop their memorization skills.

Materials

12 index cards,
8" × 10"
4 boxes
magazines
scissors (adult use
only)
glue

VOCABULARY

metal   paper   plastic   recycle

PREPARATION

- Make 12 flash cards and boxes using pictures from magazines: three with pictures of plastic items, three with pictures of metal items, three with pictures of paper items, and three with pictures of nonrecyclable items (doll, puppy, hat, and so on).
- Label boxes "plastic," "paper," or "metal"; pictures on the boxes are helpful.

WHAT TO DO

1. Engage the children in a discussion about recycling and the three types of materials that people can recycle.
2. Show the children a flash card. Identify the item. Ask, "Can it be recycled? Which bin should we place the item in?"
3. Teach the children the following fingerplay. Clap to the rhythm of the rhyme. The last line gets three strong claps.

   Toss It In by Christina Chilcote
   Toss in the plastic.
   Toss in the tin.
   Toss in the paper.
   Toss it in!

TEACHER-TO-TEACHER TIP

- While real items can be used instead of pictures, make sure metal objects have no sharp edges.

ASSESSMENT

Consider the following:
- After the group practice, can each child identify if an item should be recycled?
- Can the children determine which bin each item should go in?

Children's Books

*Recycle!: a Handbook
for Kids* by
Gail Gibbons
*Stuff: Reduce, Reuse,
Recycle* by Steven Kroll
*Why Should I Recycle
Garbage?* by
M. J. Knight

Christina Chilcote, New Freedom, PA

The Greenhouse

LEARNING OBJECTIVES

The children will:
1. Understand how to plant and care for plants.
2. Develop social skills as they work together using common materials.

Materials

small stand-alone
   water table
potting soil (fertilizer
   free)
variety of seeds
plastic garden tools:
   rakes, trowels, and
   spades
watering cans
gardening gloves (4
   pairs)
aprons
sun hats
sunglasses
small boxes
shredded brown
   paper bags
plastic vegetables
dried or plastic flowers
plastic flower vases

VOCABULARY

flowers	harvest	rake	trowel
garden gloves	plant	seed	vegetable
greenhouse	potting soil	spade	watering can

WHAT TO DO

1. Have the children help you set up a fun and fancy greenhouse in your dramatic play area.
2. Set up a small water table in which the children can plant real seeds in real potting soil. When potted, the seeds can be put on a sunny windowsill or taken outside.
3. Add gardening tools such as spades, rakes, trowels, watering cans, and garden gloves. Also add gardening clothes such as aprons, hats, and sunglasses.
4. Place small boxes on low tables. Add shredded brown paper bags to the boxes to simulate dirt. The children can "plant" the plastic foods usually found in the Dramatic Play center and "harvest" them using the trowels and rakes.
5. Add dried or plastic flowers. These also can be "planted" in the gardening boxes.
6. Add plastic flower vases so the children can "cut" their flowers and make arrangements.

ASSESSMENT

Consider the following:
- Show the children photos of a variety of plants. Ask them what those plants need in order to survive.
- Observe the children carefully as they play in the Greenhouse. Do they share equipment easily or do they hoard items? Are real conversations happening? Are the children playing interactively or involved mostly in parallel play?

Virginia Jean Herrod, Columbia, SC

Children's Books

Abuelito's Greenhouse
   by Susan Ring
*Mr. Percy's Magic
   Greenhouse* by
   Anthea Kemp
*Out and About at
   the Greenhouse* by
   Bitsy Kemper

Recycling Relay

LEARNING OBJECTIVES

The children will:
1. Improve their large motor skills.
2. Cooperate with partners.
3. Improve their understanding about recycling.

Materials

4 recycle bins
   (rectangular,
   approximately
   2' × 3')
various materials
   for recycling,
   including
   cardboard,
   plastic, glass,
   newspaper,
   paper,
   aluminum,
   metal, and so on

VOCABULARY

aluminum	collect	metal	plastic
cardboard	glass	paper	recycle bin

PREPARATION

- Display the four recycling bins at one end of the room.
- Display a set of five or more items in a row ahead of each bin. Leave five or more feet of space between each item.

WHAT TO DO

1. Divide the class into four teams.
2. Assign each child a partner within the team.
3. Have partners line up behind their bin.
4. One child will push the bin while the other child collects recyclables along the way.
5. On the command of "ready, set, recycle!" the four pairs of children push their bins down the length of the room, collecting and naming the recyclables as they place them in their bin.
6. The team players then touch the wall on the opposite side of the room and push the bin back to their team.
7. After the relay, remove the items and display them in rows again, ready for the next group of children. As you remove and display items, invite the children to identify each type of recyclable and chant the word aloud: "aluminum," "cardboard," "plastic," and so on.

ASSESSMENT

Consider the following:
- Can the children identify the items set out and say whether they are recyclable?
- Display an assortment of recyclables on a table. Invite each child to come forward and select an item. Have the child tell how he could reuse the item before recycling it.

Children's Books

How on Earth Do We Recycle Plastic? by Janet D'Amato
Recycle!: A Handbook for Kids by Gail Gibbons
Stuff: Reduce, Reuse, Recycle by Steven Kroll

Mary J. Murray, Mazomanie, WI

The Earth Ball Game

4+

The children will:

1. Identify the colors associated with the different components of our planet—soil (brown), grass and leaves (green), water (blue), sky (blue), sun (yellow) and flowers (for example, red).
2. Develop their large motor skills.

Materials

inflatable rubber globe or a 10"–12" ball
nontoxic paints (blue, green, brown)
paintbrush
magazines
tagboard

VOCABULARY

blue	Earth	leaves	soil
brown	green	red	yellow

PREPARATION

- Inflate the globe or paint a ball to simulate Earth with blue and green (or brown) paint.
- Using magazine pictures on tagboard, make an 8" x 10" flash card for each of the Earth components: soil, grass and leaves, the sun, the ocean, the sky with clouds, and a red flower.

WHAT TO DO

1. Identify each flash card with the class. Explain that they are an important part of Earth.
2. Ask the color of the object. Have the children repeat the color.
3. Join the class sitting in a circle on the floor. Roll the ball to one child while asking everyone, "What color is soil?"
4. Repeat the color with the children. Ask the selected child to roll the ball back to you.
5. Go through each item and color until every child has had a turn catching and returning "Earth."

TEACHER-TO-TEACHER TIP

- After the joint class responses, call the children by name and ask what the color of a particular item is as you roll the ball to them: "Audrey, what is the color of the sky?"

ASSESSMENT

Consider the following:

- Can the children associate the correct color with each Earth component?
- Does each child have the motor skill to catch and roll the Earth Ball?

Children's Books

All New Crafts for Earth Day by Kathy Ross
It's Earth Day! by Mercer Mayer
Our Earth: Making Less Trash by Peggy Hock
Reusing Things by Susan Barraclough

Christina Chilcote, New Freedom, PA

Garbage Gobble Catch

LEARNING OBJECTIVES

The children will:
1. Develop their small and large motor skills.
2. Demonstrate their ability to follow instructions to play the game.

Materials

empty milk jugs
heavy-duty scissors
  (adult use only)
markers
scrap/used paper
  such as extra
  worksheets

VOCABULARY

face	garbage	partner	reduce	scoop	trash
game	gobble	recycle	reuse	throw	

PREPARATION

● Wash out milk jugs and cut off the base so that you have a scoop.
● Draw a face on your scoop so that the opening looks like a wide open mouth.

WHAT TO DO

1. Explain there are three ways to make less trash.
   ● We can use less that needs to be thrown away (reduce).
   ● We can use things again (reuse).
   ● We can send them to a place that will make them into new things (recycle).
   Tell the children to "gobble up" all that trash, you will make a garbage gobbling game.
2. Give each child a scoop. Have them draw faces on their jugs, and show them the one you drew as an example.
3. Have each child take a piece of scrap/used paper and wad it up into a ball.
4. Divide the class into pairs. Have one child from each pair drop a wad of paper into the scoop. This child will use the scoop to throw the paper to a partner.
5. The second child will catch the paper, gobbling it up.
6. Allow the children to play for a set time, assisting as needed.

Children's Books

Recycle by
Gail Gibbons
Recycle Every Day by
Nancy Elizabeth
Wallace
Recycled! by
Jillian Powell

ASSESSMENT

Consider the following:
● Are the children able to decorate the scoop?
● Are the children able to follow the instructions for the game?
● Are the children able to catch and throw the paper?

Sue Bradford Edwards, Florissant, MO

Mother Earth Says

4+

LEARNING OBJECTIVES

The children will:
1. Demonstrate ability to play a game.
2. Stay with an activity for a reasonable length of time.
3. Follow simple commands.

Materials

tagboard
marker
child-safe scissors
container

VOCABULARY

eyes	mouth	point	wave
foot	nose	sit	whisper
head	open	touch	wiggle

PREPARATION

- Print simple commands on tagboard to make calling cards for a game similar to "Simon Says." Place them in a container.

WHAT TO DO

1. Explain to the children that is a game like "Simon Says" but it is called "Mother Earth Says."
2. When you say "Mother Earth Says" and a command card is read, the children are to follow the command all at once.
3. The children are to remain still if you do not say "Mother Earth Says" before reading a command card.

SONG

Sing "It's a Small World" with the children.

ASSESSMENT

Consider the following:
- Do the children show an increase in their ability to listen?
- Do the children understand how to play the game?
- Do the children show interest in the activity?

Jackie Wright, Enid, OK

Children's Books

Grover's 10 Terrific Ways to Help Our Wonderful World by Anna Ross
Our Earth by Anne Rockwell
We Share One World by Jane E. Hoffelt

Recycle to Make a New Toy 4+

LEARNING OBJECTIVES

The children will:

1. Learn that recycling can get them a new toy.
2. Improve their fine motor skills and manipulation.
3. Practice following directions.

Materials

scissors (adult use
  only)
small plastic bottles
sandpaper
strips of paper
string
decorating
  materials
glue
aluminum foil
tape

VOCABULARY

ball   cup   recycle   toy   Victorian

PREPARATION

- Cut the bottoms off plastic bottles.
- Smooth the cut edges with sandpaper.
- Cut papers to fit around the bottles.
- Cut string to 18" lengths.

WHAT TO DO

1. Give each child a piece of precut paper and encourage them to decorate it.
2. While they work, tell them about toys from Victorian times, for example, hoops, tops, and the cup and ball, which is what they are making.
3. When decorated and dry, glue the decorated papers around the bottles.
4. Help the children tie the string around the bottle neck.
5. Lay the end of the string on a strip of aluminium foil and tape it on.
6. Crunch the foil up into a tight ball and wind tape around this.
7. Show the children how to hold the bottle by the neck with the ball of foil hanging loose. Then jerk your arm, tossing the ball above the bottle, trying to catch it in the cup.
8. Remind them to keep their eye on the ball!

TEACHER-TO-TEACHER TIP

- Although younger children can make the toy, they often lack the coordination to get the ball into the cup.

ASSESSMENT

Consider the following:

- Do the children understand the concept that the bottle will become a toy?
- How well do the children follow instructions?
- Ask the children why we should recycle.

Children's Books

*The Adventures of a
Plastic Bottle* by
Alison Inches
*The Three Rs: Reuse,
Reduce, Recycle* by
Nuria Roca
Why Should I Recycle?
by Jen Green

Anne Adeney, Plymouth, United Kingdom

Small World, Big Words

3+

LEARNING OBJECTIVES

The children will:
1. Explore various natural objects.
2. Learn to use descriptive words in relation to natural objects.

Materials

magnifying glasses
chart paper
markers

VOCABULARY

bumpy	forest	observe	sand	sparkly
describe	glittery	playground	shiny	
filled	nature	rough	smooth	

WHAT TO DO

1. Choose an area to observe, anywhere from a field or forest to the playground.
2. Show the children how to hold a magnifying glass close to an object for observation. Looking closely at pebbles, sand, and plants are good beginning activities.
3. Invite the children to take turns using words to describe their small objects: for example, "Pebbles look sparkly, glittery, and shiny."
4. Challenge the children to use new or different words each time. Some may even want to make up their own descriptive words.
5. Record the words on paper to keep track of the variety of words and to use for comparing objects later.

TEACHER-TO-TEACHER TIPS

- Ask each child to think of an object without telling anyone what it is. The children can then take turns describing their secret objects until someone guesses the item's identity. For example, a child whose chosen item is a rock could say, "My object is red, rough, glittery, hard, and small."
- Create a chart showing words the children use to describe each object:

Pebble	Leaf	Flower	Ant	Twig
shiny	smooth	colorful	wiggly	rough
hard	fuzzy	smooth	round	long
rough	jagged		small	bumpy
smooth				

Children's Books

The Earth and I by Frank Asch
Our Earth by Anne Rockwell
We Share One World by Jane E. Hoffelt

ASSESSMENT

Consider the following:
- Are the children able to use terms that describe the natural objects?
- Do the children think of their own terms, or rely on terms you or other children suggested?

Karen Johnson, Grand Rapids, MI

A to Z: Let's Go Green!

5+

LEARNING OBJECTIVES

The children will:

1. Learn about many ways to care for the Earth.
2. Learn letter sounds and the alphabet.

Materials

poster board
marker

VOCABULARY

alphabet   care   conservation

WHAT TO DO

1. Make a large poster that has an A to Z list of ideas for how to help the Earth.
   Here are some examples:
   - **B**icycle instead of using a car.
   - **D**on't run the water when brushing your teeth.
   - **E**at organic foods.
   - **F**eed the birds.
   - **G**row a flower or vegetable garden.
   - **P**lant a tree.
   - **Q**uit wasting food.
   - **R**educe, Reuse, Recycle!
   - **T**urn off the lights.
   - **U**se paper on both sides.

2. As you teach each letter, introduce a green idea, a green project, and sing the following song:

   Whole World Green by Kathy Stemke
   (Tune: "Mary Had a Little Lamb")
   I will make my whole world green,   *I will make my whole world green.*
   Whole world green, whole world green,   *G-R-E-E-N, green!*

3. The following are some examples of green ideas and green projects. Challenge the children to think of some of their own:
   - Feed the birds: Make a bird feeder.
   - Grow a garden: Make a tin-can herb garden.
   - Hold on to helium balloons: Make a helium balloon craft.
   - Join your friends to clean up your neighborhood: Make a trash monster.
   - Plant a tree: Make a thankful tree.
   - Reduce, Reuse, Recycle: Use old ice cream containers as building blocks.
   - Visit a recycling center: Become a human recycling machine.

ASSESSMENT

Consider the following:
- Can the children name some ways to care for the Earth?
- Are the children able to memorize the song?

Children's Books

Our Earth by Anne Rockwell
Reduce, Reuse, Recycle Plastic by Alexandra Fix
We Share One World by Jane E. Hoffelt

Kathy Stemke, Mount Airy, GA

The Three Rs Poster Collages

5+

LEARNING OBJECTIVES

The children will:
1. Identify items which can be reduced, reused, or recycled.
2. Develop social skills as they work together on a group project.

VOCABULARY

manufacture	recycle	reuse
nature	reduce	sort

PREPARATION

- Use the black marker to make a large uppercase R on the three pieces of poster board.
- Cut out the three Rs and set them in different work spaces: one labeled "reduce," one labeled "reuse," and one labeled "recycle."

WHAT TO DO

1. Engage the children in a discussion about recycling.
2. Help the children sort magazine pictures into the three categories. Put the pictures on the appropriate work spaces.
3. Explain that manufactured items are not the only things filling up our landfills. Add natural items such as leaves, grass, and small twigs. Discuss how to reuse or recycle these items.
4. Have the children paint over the letters with a heavy glue wash, then apply the pictures and other materials to the appropriate R.
5. As you work, talk to the children about the concepts of the three Rs.
6. Display the three Rs on a bulletin board with an appropriate heading.

ASSESSMENT

Consider the following:
- Can the children look at images of materials and say whether they are recyclable or reusable?
- As the children work together, observe those who find sharing materials easy and those who still try to hoard items for their own use.

Virginia Jean Herrod, Columbia, SC

Materials

thick black permanent marker
3 large pieces of poster board
magazine pictures of a variety of items (paper, plastic, glass, and food)
newspapers
junk mail with the address removed or blacked out
natural items such as leaves, grass, and twigs
glue
paintbrushes

Children's Books

Recycling: Learning the Four Rs: Reduce, Reuse, Recycle, Recover by Martin J. Gutnik
Reduce, Reuse, Recycle Plastic by Alexandra Fix
Stuff! Reduce, Reuse, Recycle by Steven Kroll
The Three Rs: Reuse, Reduce, Recycle by Nuria Roca

Reuse! Obstacle Course

LEARNING OBJECTIVES

The children will:

1. Improve their large motor skills.
2. Follow directions.
3. Learn about recycling.

Materials

cardboard boxes of
    varying sizes
plastic laundry
    detergent jugs or
    gallon milk jugs
bundles of
    newspaper
recycling bins
aluminum cans
kite string
collection of smaller
    recyclables such
    as aluminum
    cans, plastic
    yogurt
    containers, water
    bottles, and so on

VOCABULARY

around	carry	finish	over	start	under
between	course	obstacle	recycle	through	

PREPARATION

- Create an obstacle course in the classroom using the materials listed to the left. Label a "start" and a "finish."

WHAT TO DO

1. Invite the children to observe the obstacle course you set up.
2. Encourage the children to comment on the materials you have in the obstacle course and what each item was previously used for. Ask the children to use these sentences as they share their comments.

   This _____ used to be for _____.
   Now it_____.

3. Draw the children's attention to the end of the obstacle course. Explain that after the children move through the course they are to select one item from the collection of recyclables and place it in the recycling bin.
4. Demonstrate how to move through the obstacle course moving over, under, through, between, and so on from start to finish.
5. Invite the children to line up and do the same. Encourage the children to move through the course several times.
6. Gather the children together and invite them to think of ways to rearrange the reusable materials to create a new obstacle course, and then repeat the activity.

ASSESSMENT

Consider the following:

- Can the children identify the previous uses of the materials that make up the obstacle course?
- How well do the children navigate the obstacle course?

Children's Books

The Great Trash Bash by
    Loreen Leedy
*Recycle! A Handbook
    for Kids* by
    Gail Gibbons
*Stuff! Reduce, Reuse,
    Recycle* by Steven Kroll

Mary J. Murray, Mazomanie, WI

Save a Tree: Use Less Paper

4+

LEARNING OBJECTIVES

The children will:
1. Improve their sense of balance.
2. Verbalize about using less paper and not wasting paper.
3. Improve their oral language skills.
4. Improve their critical-thinking skills.

Materials

picture of a tree
balance beam
tissue box
paper towel roll
cardboard box
envelopes
paper
cardboard tubes
paper plates
napkins
paper cups

VOCABULARY

balance	conserve	protect	save	use
beam	paper	resource	tree	

PREPARATION

- Display the picture of a tree at one end of the balance beam.
- Display the collection of paper products at the other end of the balance beam.

WHAT TO DO

1. Remind the children that paper comes from trees, and that the more paper we use, the more trees have to be cut down.
2. Talk with the children about the importance of using fewer paper products as a way of caring for our Earth.
3. Display the various items listed under "materials" and invite the children to share what they can do to conserve paper.
4. Remind the children they can use fewer paper products or use something in place of each paper product.
5. Demonstrate how to pick up one of the paper products and carry it across the balance beam, then set the item down by the picture of the tree.
6. As you display the item near the tree picture, recite the following: "I will use less paper. I will save more trees."
7. Invite the children to pick up an item and repeat the process you modeled.
8. Repeat the activity with more materials.

Children's Books

Living in a Forest by Patty Whitehouse
Reduce, Reuse, Recycle Plastic by Alexandra Fix
Paper by Kate Walker

ASSESSMENT

Consider the following:
- Do the children make the connection between paper and trees?
- Listen and assess the children's understanding and oral language skills as the children do the activity.

Mary J. Murray, Mazomanie, WI

Charting Plant Growth

3

LEARNING OBJECTIVES

The children will:
1. Chart the growth of their seeds.
2. Compare the growth of different varieties of plants.

Materials

scissors (adult use only)

plastic bottles

seeds for fast-growing plants, such as grass or sprouts

soil

plant growth charts for each child and adult

rulers

growth chart used for children

VOCABULARY

| chart | grow | measure | ruler | seeds |
| compare | height | plant | soil | |

PREPARATION

● Cut off the tops of plastic bottles to make recycled planters. Poke holes in the bottom with scissors.

WHAT TO DO

1. Help the children add soil and seeds to their recycled planters. Once most of the plants have begun to grow, hold up the growth chart used for children.
2. Ask if any children have one at home and demonstrate its use by measuring a few children.
3. Tell the children they will chart the growth of their plants every week. Demonstrate how to measure your plant and fill in the height on your plant chart.
4. Allow the children to practice with the rulers and assist them with measuring and charting their plants.
5. Continue charting each week. After two to three weeks, have each child present his chart to the class.
6. Discuss whether any plants are growing more rapidly than others. Are any varieties faster growers? Repeat this process after another week or two.

TEACHER-TO-TEACHER TIP

● Charting plant growth must be done over a long enough period for results to be clear to the children. The necessary time depends on the varieties of seeds and other growing conditions. You can also chart the number of leaves on each plant.

ASSESSMENT

Consider the following:
● Can the children chart plant growth accurately?
● Do the children recognize that some plants grow faster than others?

Children's Books

The Carrot Seed by Ruth Kraus
Out and About at the Greenhouse by Bitsy Kemper
Planting a Rainbow by Lois Ehlert
Tops and Bottoms by Janet Stevens

Debbie Vilardi, Commack, NY

Grocery Shopping

LEARNING OBJECTIVES

The children will:
1. Improve their number identification skills.
2. Review numerical order.
3. Become familiar with role playing.

Materials

containers
3 reusable
   shopping bags
15 or more plastic,
   glass, cardboard,
   or aluminum
   containers from
   grocery and
   household
   products
black bold line
   marker

VOCABULARY

bag	grocery	recycle	shop
buy	number	sequence	

PREPARATION

- Write a number between 1–5 on each object so there are three sets of five objects. Put the objects in containers, also labeled 1–5.
- Display the containers randomly on a table or shelf to create a "store."
- Display a sign that reads "Store" at the table.

WHAT TO DO

1. Remind the children that when we grocery shop we can also help take care of our Earth.
2. Explain that many items we purchase at grocery stores come in containers that can be recycled.
3. Display the reusable shopping bags and share how people can use special reusable grocery bags in place of paper bags, and how this can save trees.
4. Invite one or more of the children to "go shopping" at the table of containers.
5. Instruct the children to select items with numbers from 1–5 and put them in their shopping bags.
6. Have each child carry his bag of items to another area of the classroom and remove the items from the bag.
7. Invite the child to identify each number again and then sequence the items from 1–5, in a row across the floor or table.
8. Give the child a round of applause and then have the child return the items to the "grocery store."

ASSESSMENT

Consider the following:
- Are the children able to select items with the numbers 1–5 on them?
- Can the children place the items in correct numerical order?

Children's Books

Bob the Builder: Bob's Recycling Day by Annie Auerbach
The Great Recycling Adventure by Jan McHarry
Recycling by Rhonda Lucas Donald

Mary J. Murray, Mazomanie, WI

Hopping Bird!

4+

LEARNING OBJECTIVES

The children will:
1. Learn about numbers and "odd" and "even."
2. Learn to identify shapes by their names.
3. Improve their motor skills.

Materials

images of birds
scraps of light-
   colored vinyl
   material
scissors (adult use
   only)
black permanent
   marker or black
   electrical tape
masking tape

VOCABULARY

even   odd   skip count

PREPARATION

- Cut different shapes out of the vinyl scraps (square, triangle, rectangle, circle, oval, and so on).
- Make the shapes large enough for children to jump on.
- Use either black permanent marker or black tape to number the shapes.
- Tape the shapes to the floor with masking tape to prevent accidents.
- Discuss how little birds hop around instead of walk.

WHAT TO DO

1. Engage the children in a conversation about birds. Show the children images of various birds. Explain to the children that birds are an important part of the Earth's environment, and that a way to care for birds is to respect the environment.
2. Challenge the children to identify some of the birds you have images of, and describe for the children those birds' various habitats (penguins, flamingos, and parrots are interesting examples).
3. Tell the children to act like little hopping birds! Encourage them to try the following:
   - Jump on each shape and identify it.
   - Walk on each shape and say the number.
   - Jump from 1–10, saying each number as you go.
   - Jump on the even numbers only.
   - Jump on the odd numbers only.
   - Skip jump by fives. (5, 10, 15, 20, 25…)
   - Skip jump by tens. (10, 20, 30…)
   - Skip jump by twos or threes.
   - Walk backwards on the shapes and count backwards.
   - Jump and recite the numbers backwards.
   - Hop on one foot.
   - Jump hands on the shape then the feet on the shape.

ASSESSMENT

Consider the following:
- Can the children identify the shapes by name?
- How successful are the children at counting in the various ways?

Kathy Stemke, Mount Airy, GA

Children's Books

Living in a Forest by
   Patty Whitehouse
The Tree by Dana Lyons
What's a Jaybird to Do?
   by Cat Sauer

Milk-Lid Patterns

4+

LEARNING OBJECTIVES

The children will:

1. Identify shapes and colors.
2. Identify and continue simple patterns.

Materials

clean milk bottle
lids in a variety of
colors

VOCABULARY

color words   lid   pattern   round   shape

WHAT TO DO

1. Reuse milk bottle lids by placing them in the math center. Ask the children what shape the lids are. Have the children name the colors of the lids.
2. Arrange the lids into an ABAB pattern using two of the colors. Have the children continue the pattern.
3. Using the same colors, create an AABAAB pattern, and have the children continue the pattern.
4. Create an ABCABC pattern using three colors, and have the children continue the pattern.
5. Begin different patterns for the children to continue, and then have them design their own patterns.

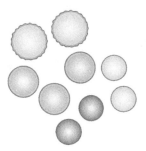
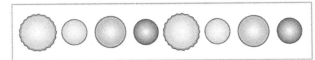

TEACHER-TO-TEACHER TIP

● Have the children bring clean, empty milk bottles with lids from home the week before you plan on doing this activity. Collect the lids for the math center to show the children that the lids can be reused. Recycle the bottles, or see how else you can use them in the classroom.

ASSESSMENT

Consider the following:

● Are the children able to identify the shape and colors of the lids?
● Can the children identify and continue simple patterns?

Children's Books

Recycle Every Day! by
Nancy Elizabeth
Wallace
*The Three Rs: Reuse,
Reduce, Recycle* by
Nuria Roca
Why Should I Recycle?
by Jen Green

Laura Wynkoop, San Dimas, CA

Ocean Play

LEARNING OBJECTIVES

The children will:

1. Learn about things that live and belong in the ocean.
2. Develop their ability to create and reproduce patterns.

Materials

large sheet of blue
   paper
seashells
toy fish and sea
   creatures
images of things
   that belong in
   the ocean

VOCABULARY

crab	fish	ocean	recreate	starfish
create	lobster	pattern	skill	

WHAT TO DO

1. Set out blue paper and several seashells, toy fish, and images of ocean objects.
2. Engage the children in a discussion about objects that come from the ocean, about all the things that live in the ocean, and why it is important to care for the ocean.
3. Invite the children to create, extend, and reproduce patterns using seashells, fish, and ocean objects.

TEACHER-TO-TEACHER TIP

- For more advanced children, create more difficult patterns and challenge the children to recreate the patterns and designs.

ASSESSMENT

Consider the following:

- How well do the children recreate the patterns of the ocean creatures?
- Do the children understand the difference between what belongs in the ocean and what does not, and why it is important to keep the ocean clean?

Mary J. Murray, Mazomanie, WI

Children's Books

Beaches by
Emma Bernay
*Do You Know About
Life in the Sea?* by
Philip Steele
*The Ocean Alphabet
Book* by Jerry Pallotta

Recycling Adds Up!

4+

LEARNING OBJECTIVES

The children will:
1. Learn number recognition.
2. Become familiar with sorting, sets, and counting.

Materials

variety of plastic objects with recycling symbols and numbers stamped on them

VOCABULARY

count	recycle	reuse	sort
numbers	reduce	sets	symbol

PREPARATION

- Ahead of time, discuss the symbol/numbering system with the children. Show them images or examples of recycling symbols.
- Set the plastic objects on a table for easy sorting. Record the correct amount for each sorted number set so you can check the children's work.

WHAT TO DO

1. Ask the children to sort the objects by the recycling number stamped on the side or the bottom.
2. Once they are finished, help them count the number of items in each set and compare this to the list you made.
3. After that, help them count the total number of items. The children can do this project independently or in a group.

TEACHER-TO-TEACHER TIPS

- For older children, write beginning equations. For instance, the sets can be added in the following way: 3 objects + 2 objects = 5 objects.
- Adding nonrecyclables provides an extra challenge.

Children's Books

Recycle Every Day! by Nancy Elizabeth Wallace
Reusing and Recycling by Charlotte Guillain
The Three Rs: Reuse, Reduce, Recycle by Nuria Roca
Why Should I Recycle? by Jen Green

ASSESSMENT

Consider the following:
- Are the children able to look for the symbols and numbers? Are they able to sort the plastics?
- Do the younger children practice number recognition, sorting, set formation, and counting?
- Are the older children able to solve any of the equations?

Monica Shaughnessy, Katy, TX

How Much Trash Do We Make?

5+

LEARNING OBJECTIVES

The children will:
1. Learn the meaning of recycling-related terms.
2. Learn about trash and recycling.

Materials

roll of clear contact
   paper
tape
permanent marker

VOCABULARY

compare	equal	more	trash
count	least	recyclable	waste
environment	less	recycle	

WHAT TO DO

1. This activity will start on Monday and end on Friday. On Monday, cut a large strip of clear contact paper, remove the backing, and tape it to the wall, sticky-side out. Write "Monday" on the top.
2. Tell the children that you will be collecting trash all day so each time they have trash they need to stick it to the contact paper. Include paper towels from hand washing, snack and lunch trash (but no food waste), and art trash.
3. At the end of the day put another piece of clear contact paper over the trash and have the children help you count out all the trash. Talk about ways that you could have made less trash: for example, using one paper towel when drying hands, putting food in washable items, or using reusable items.
4. Do this activity each day for a week. Compare the days and talk about which day had the most trash, which had the least, and if any days were equal. Hopefully, by Friday the trash collection will be a lot less.
5. Hang these where parents can see how much trash the class made each day.

TEACHER-TO-TEACHER TIP

- After doing this experiment, a field trip to your local recycling center is very well received, because the children are now aware of how much trash they contribute to our world.

ASSESSMENT

Consider the following:
- Have the children write or dictate to you a letter to the school or their parents about ways to make less trash.
- Can the children indicate which day had the most trash and which had the least?

Children's Books

Recycle Every Day by Nancy Elizabeth Wallace
Reduce, Reuse, Recycle Plastic by Alexandra Fix
We Share One World by Jane E. Hoffelt

Holly Dzieranowski, Brenham, TX

Drumming Up Fun

LEARNING OBJECTIVES

The children will:
1. Develop an appreciation of music.
2. Practice keeping time to a rhythm.
3. Improve their creative art skills.

Materials

construction paper
scissors (adult use
  only)
tape
coffee cans with
  lids
cylindrical oatmeal
  containers with
  lids
art supplies

VOCABULARY

beat	create	drum	reuse
container	decorate	hit	rhythm

PREPARATION

- Ahead of time, send home a letter inviting the children's families to begin collecting coffee cans and oatmeal containers for the activity.
- Cut construction paper to fit the cans and containers, wrap it around the containers, and secure it with tape.

WHAT TO DO

1. Talk with the children about reusing things instead of throwing them away.
2. Display a coffee can or oatmeal container. Ask the children to think of something they could reuse the container for. Allow time for the children to share their responses.
3. Explain that the children will make their own drums using similar containers.
4. Display pages from the suggested books to demonstrate ways to create instruments from common household items.
5. Provide each child with a paper-wrapped "drum" and art supplies.
6. Invite the children to use the art supplies to decorate their drums. When the children finish creating their drums, gather them together.
7. Invite the children to keep the beat as you play various rhythms on your drum and they follow along.
8. Play a favorite class song and ask the children to sing along and play their drums.
9. Remind the children while they enjoy their drums to think about how they helped care for the Earth by reusing something that might have been thrown away.

ASSESSMENT

Consider the following:
- How well do the children decorate their drums?
- How well do the children play their drums while singing a favorite song?

Children's Books

Making Music by
Josie Stewart and
Lynn Salem
*Musical Instruments
You Can Make* by
Phyllis Hayes
Pluck and Scrape by
Sally Hewitt

Mary J. Murray, Mazomanie, WI

Recycling Band

4+

LEARNING OBJECTIVES

The children will:

1. Use rhythm instruments.
2. Create rhythm instruments.
3. Sing and march together.
4. Learn the benefit of reusing and recycling materials.

Materials

rhythm instruments
various recyclable
    materials such as
    plastic jugs,
    aluminum or
    metal cans,
    cardboard boxes
    and containers in
    various shapes,
    plastic or glass
    containers with
    lids, metal
    spoons, dried
    beans
music about
    recycling, or
    other favorite
    songs

VOCABULARY

beat	instrument	recycle	shaker
drum	march	reuse	sing
horn	music	rhythm	song

WHAT TO DO

1. Display several rhythm instruments as you demonstrate how each one makes a different sound.
2. Display the assorted recyclables on a table. Talk with the children about reusing the materials to create new rhythm instruments.
3. Guide the children in creating a simple rhythm instrument using the materials.
4. Help the children fill small glass or plastic containers with a handful of dried beans then attach the lid to create a "shaker." Use an aluminum can and a spoon as a drum. Use an oatmeal container with a lid as a bongo drum. Use a cardboard tube like a horn.
5. Encourage creativity as the children experiment and make music with the instruments.
6. Invite the children to form a single- or double-file line as they carry their newly created instruments.
7. Play a favorite recycling song and invite the class to march around the room, keeping the beat and singing along as you celebrate taking care of our Earth.

Children's Books

Let's Recycle by
Anne L. Mackenzie
*We Are Extremely Very
Good Recyclers* by
Lauren Child
*Why Should I
Recycle Garbage?* by
M. J. Knight

ASSESSMENT

Consider the following:

- How well do the children keep the beat with the instruments?
- Can the children follow specific instructions with their instruments?
- Do the children recognize the recycling aspect of this activity?

Mary J. Murray, Mazomanie, WI

Nature Walk

4+

LEARNING OBJECTIVES

The children will:
1. Learn about classification, counting, shapes, and sorting.
2. Develop their small motor skills.
3. Learn about various parts of nature.

Materials

colorful paper
  plates
1" or wider 2-sided
  tape
markers

VOCABULARY

discovery	leaves	pebbles	shape
grass	nature	seeds	walk
identity	outdoor		

WHAT TO DO

1. Attach two or more strips of the two-sided tape to each plate.
2. Give each child a sticky plate and take them outdoors for a nature walk.
3. Invite the children to collect a variety of interesting objects on the walk. The children may collect seeds, leaves, pebbles, blades of grass, and so on.
4. Have the children "stick" each item to their plate.
5. After the children have collected an assortment of items, invite them to sit in a circle and tell the group about what they collected.
6. Encourage the children to identify the shape of each item, how many items they have, and how certain items could be grouped together.
7. Back in the classroom, let the children record what they found by drawing each item on another paper plate. Help them write words for each of the objects or shapes.

Children's Books

The Earth and I by
  Frank Asch
Our Earth by
  Anne Rockwell
We Share One World
  by Jane E. Hoffelt

ASSESSMENT

Consider the following:
- Can the children describe the differences between various items taken from nature?
- Can the children recall where they discovered the various natural materials?

Mary J. Murray, Mazomanie, WI

Nothing but Sand

4+

LEARNING OBJECTIVES

The children will:
1. Learn the importance of keeping our beaches clean.
2. Use tools to clean the sand in the sand table.
3. Develop small and large motor skills.

Materials

sand table
shovels
strainers
pails
litter (clean bottle caps, scraps of paper, aluminum foil, gum wrappers, plastic rings from a six-pack of soda, and so on)

VOCABULARY

beach	healthy	sand	strainer
clean	litter	shovel	trash
dirty	pail		

PREPARATION

● Bury the litter in the sand table.

WHAT TO DO

1. Ask the children if they have ever been to the beach. Did they see litter in the sand?
   Tell the children that litter makes our beaches and oceans dirty. It can hurt fish, birds, and other sea animals. Explain that animals sometimes eat litter because they mistake it for food, and it can make them very sick. It is important to keep our beaches clean so that our planet can be healthy.
2. Have the children pretend that the sand table is a beach. Ask the children to use the shovels and strainers to clean up the litter in the sand. They can collect the litter in the pails. Have the children continue until the only thing left in the table is the sand.

TEACHER-TO-TEACHER TIP

● The third Saturday of September is Coastal Cleanup Day. More than 60 nations participate in this annual event to clean up the shores along oceans, lakes, and rivers. Encourage the children and their families to take part in the largest volunteer day on the planet.

ASSESSMENT

Consider the following:
● Ask the children why we should keep our beaches clean.
● Can the children use tools to remove litter from the sand in the sand table?

Children's Books

Beaches by Emma Bernay
Beaches by JoAnn Early Macken
Blue Bug's Beach Party by Virginia Poulet

Laura Wynkoop, San Dimas, CA

Planting Trees

4+

LEARNING OBJECTIVES

The children will:

1. Develop an understanding of the value of trees.
2. Develop their oral language skills.
3. Expand their vocabulary.

Materials

twigs or branches
  from trees
sand
sand table

VOCABULARY

animals	dirt	lumber	shade	tree
birds	Earth	paper	sun	water
climb	fruit	plant		

WHAT TO DO

1. Talk with the children about the value and beauty of trees. Be sure to mention that trees give us paper, fruit, lumber, nuts, shade, a place to climb, and places for animals to live. They also help keep our air clean by producing carbon dioxide.
2. Invite the children to share what they know or appreciate about trees.
3. Direct the children's attention to the sand table. Invite two children to role play planting trees as they insert each "tree" into the sand, to create a forest of trees in the sand table.
4. Encourage the children to talk among themselves as they work about how important trees are and how we can take care of the Earth by planting trees.
5. After the first two children are finished, allow time for several more pairs of children to work and play at the sand table.
6. Remind the children to remove all the "trees" before they leave the table so that it is ready for the next pair of children.

TEACHER-TO-TEACHER TIP

- If possible, take the children outdoors and sit beneath a tree as you introduce this activity and read aloud one of the books listed with this activity.
- Invite the children to paint pictures of trees. Ask the children to verbalize what they know about trees. Record their words on the completed page of artwork. Display them in the classroom.

Children's Books

The Lorax by Dr. Seuss
The Tree by Dana Lyons
Trees by David Burnie

ASSESSMENT

Consider the following:

- Do the children indicate an understanding of the importance of trees?
- Can the children describe some of the things that trees provide for us?

Mary J. Murray, Mazomanie, WI

Water, Water, Where Is the Water?

LEARNING OBJECTIVES

The children will:
1. Use their senses to explore and observe materials and natural phenomena.
2. Make predictions about what will happen next.

Materials

several dishpans
  filled halfway
  with dry sand
jugs of water
chart paper
markers
various plastic cups
  and jars
Our Earth by Anne
  Rockwell

VOCABULARY

downpour	gush	rain	stream
flood	overflow	sand	water
force	pour		

PREPARATION

● Fill several dishpans halfway with sand, high on one end and low on the other side, so that they resemble a hill or a mountain.
● Set out a gallon of water and several smaller containers of water.

WHAT TO DO

1. Ask the children to predict what will happen if a gallon of water is poured on the top of the sand mountain. Write their answers on chart paper.
2. Pour the gallon of water quickly at the top of the sandy mountain. Ask the children to talk about what they saw. Ask them why it happened.
3. In a different tub, repeat the same procedure using a half gallon container, a quart container, and a cup.
4. Explain to the children that rain can make rivers flood if we get a heavy downpour that lasts a long time, but a gentle rain can just trickle into a stream.
5. Read *Our Earth* by Anne Rockwell and take special note of the pages about water.

ASSESSMENT

Consider the following:
● Can the children repeat your actions and explain what is happening?
● Can the children predict what will happen next?

Children's Books

Living Near a River by
  Allan Fowler
*Oceans and Rivers
  in Danger* by
  Angela Royston
*What Lives in Streams
  and Rivers?* by
  Oona Gaarder-Juntti

Carol Hupp, Farmersville, IL

Compost Pile Experiment 3+

LEARNING OBJECTIVES

The children will:
1. Learn what a compost pile is.
2. Learn what kinds of things go into a compost pile.
3. Learn to throw litter in a garbage can.

Materials

2–3 clean, empty jars with lids (mayonnaise or peanut butter)
soil (enough to fill each jar half full)
small plastic bags
leaf or flower
small piece of lettuce, carrot, or coffee grounds
water

VOCABULARY

compost	grow	paper	soil
garbage	help	sail	

WHAT TO DO

1. Explain to the children that dropping paper and garbage on the ground does not help the Earth, but putting some things in the ground does.
2. Talk about compost piles with the children. Explain that compost piles help the Earth by creating rich soil. Explain that you will do an experiment to see what is good for the Earth.
3. With the children, fill each jar half full of soil. In one jar add a piece of plastic bag and cover it up. In the next add a leaf and the lettuce (or carrot or coffee grounds), add soil on top, a little water, and cover them.
4. Explain to the children that you will watch the jars over the next several weeks to see what happens.
5. Watch the jars for several weeks, uncover the items you buried, and discuss what happened.

ASSESSMENT

Consider the following:
- After discussing what happened in the jars, discuss what kinds of things might be good to put in a compost pile. Together make a list of things that would be good to put in a compost pile.
- Do the children understand the function of a compost pile?

Sue Fleischmann, Sussex, WI

Children's Books

Compost Critters by Bianca Lavies
The Everything Kids Environment Book by Sheri Amsel
What's Going on in the Compost Pile? by Rachel Shappell

Visitors

3+

LEARNING OBJECTIVES

The children will:

1. Observe creatures that visit the garden.
2. Learn that plants provide a habitat for many creatures.
3. Consider signs of creatures they haven't observed directly.

Materials

garden
paper
pencil

VOCABULARY

garden   list   names of common local creatures likely to visit your garden
habitat   listen   observe

WHAT TO DO

1. Tell the children what "observe" means, and practice making observations in the classroom. Explain that all of our senses may be used to make observations.
2. Walk to the garden. Begin your observations by listening. Make a list of what the children hear, from bees to traffic by writing down what the children say.
3. Next, look closely at the plants in your garden. List what you see. Have leaves been damaged? Is a worm or caterpillar crawling up a stem? Does a spider web link two plants? Has an animal dug up some roots?
4. Return to the classroom. Discuss what each creature was doing in the garden.
5. Hypothesize about those you could not observe directly. Note that the bees and ants are looking for food. The worms and spiders have built houses. The caterpillar may be seeking a cool shady spot.
6. Explain that many of these creatures live in the garden. It is their habitat.

TEACHER-TO-TEACHER TIP

- This is a good place to begin to discuss other things children observed, like traffic noise and trash, or to consider ways to make the garden an even better habitat.

Children's Books

Johnny and the Old Oak Tree by Rachel Peterpaul Paulson
The Snail's Spell by Joanne Ryder
The Tale of Peter Rabbit by Beatrix Potter

ASSESSMENT

Consider the following:

- How well do the children observe creatures in the garden, directly and indirectly?
- Do the children understand that the garden is a habitat for the creatures that live there?

Debbie Vilardi, Commack, NY

Worms Are Good Guys

LEARNING OBJECTIVES

The children will:
1. Learn the environmental value of earthworms.
2. Learn the effects of overuse of pesticides.

Materials

sand
moist garden soil
earthworms
plastic shovel
leaf mold or rotting
    leaves
water
clear plastic
    container, such
    as fish bowl or
    large flower vase
tape
black paper to
    wrap around
    container and
    block out light

VOCABULARY

dig	pesticides	tunnel
earthworm	sand	waste
fertilizer	soil	worm

PREPARATION

● Have earthworms as well as separate containers of sand and soil ready.

WHAT TO DO

1. Let the children view the earthworms. Discuss the importance of worms in the world. Explain that earthworms dig and mix soil, making it loose and airy for plants to grow. As they tunnel, they leave behind waste that plants use as fertilizer to make them strong.
2. Talk about how the overuse of pesticides can harm earthworms, since the pesticides leach into the soil where the worms live.
3. Using the plastic shovel, let the children help you put several 1 ½" layers of sand and soil in the clear container.
4. Place the worms on top of the soil and cover them with some rotting leaves or leaf mold.
5. Pour a little water on top to moisten the leaves. Let the children observe the striped layers of sand and soil. Tape black paper around the container and put it in a cool, dark place.
6. After a couple of days, remove the black paper and let the children see how the earthworms have mixed the soil layers.
7. Set the earthworms free and use the soil to plant marigolds to give to the children's families.

ASSESSMENT

Consider the following:
● Do the children show interest in and respect for worms they find outdoors?
● Can the children discuss the work done by worms, noting change in soil layers?

Children's Books

Compost Critters by
    Bianca Lavies
Diary of a Worm by
    Doreen Cronin
Earthdance by
    Joanne Ryder

Kay Flowers, Summerfield, OH

The Air We Breathe

4+

LEARNING OBJECTIVES

The children will:
1. Discover the interdependence of plants and animals.
2. Learn about what the body does when breathing.

Materials

balloons
pictures of lungs,
    trees, plants, and
    air pollution

VOCABULARY

animals	chest	healthy	lungs
breath	exhale	inhale	plants
breathe	fresh		

WHAT TO DO

1. Sit the children in a circle and have them take a few deep breaths with you.
2. Explain that when we breathe in, fresh air fills our lungs. The lungs are the two balloon-like spaces in our chests.
3. Now take a balloon and blow into it. Hold the air in the balloon and have the children take a deep breath, filling their lungs like this balloon.
4. Next, slowly let the air out of the balloon and have the children slowly exhale. Repeat the process several times.
5. Ask the children, "What happens if we do not breathe?" Some children might want to try inhaling deeply and holding their breath to find out. They will discover that the air they breathe is an essential part of life. We cannot live without air for much longer than a minute!
6. Show a picture of a tree. Ask the children how trees help us. Explain that trees help us breathe: When we breathe in, we are using the air that the trees have touched.
7. Next, show a picture of air pollution and let the children share. Why is this bad for people, animals, plants, and trees? How can we keep our air clean and healthy?

ASSESSMENT

Consider the following:
- Do the children understand the importance of the air?
- Are the children beginning to understand that plants help produce the air we breathe?

Patrick Mitchell, Yagoto, Nagoya, Japan

Children's Books

Earthdance by
Joanne Ryder
*Mandie and the
Windmill's Message* by
Lois Gladys Leppard
What's a Jaybird to Do?
By Cat Sauer

Clean Water

4+

LEARNING OBJECTIVES

The children will:
1. Learn about keeping water clean.
2. Learn to value the natural water in the world.
3. Improve their vocabulary.

Materials

samples of trash,
such as plastic
soda bottles,
yogurt cup lids,
plastic bags, and
so on
beach bag
beach umbrella
blue tablecloth or
bath towel
water toys, such as
shovels, pails,
beach balls, and
so on

VOCABULARY

beach	float	ocean	swim
clean	lake	river	water
fish	litter		

PREPARATION

- Place all the materials in the beach bag.
- Open the beach umbrella and set it in a special area in the classroom.
- Place the beach bag beneath the umbrella.

WHAT TO DO

1. Talk with the children about how we need to care for the Earth by keeping lakes, rivers, and oceans clean.
2. Invite the children to share their favorite activities to do while at the seaside.
3. Ask the children to share ideas about how they can care for the Earth by keeping the water clean.
4. Remove the blue towel (water) from the beach bag.
5. Display all the items on the "water."
6. Invite one child to come forward and remove the items that do not belong floating in the water.
7. Talk about how the trash and litter should be taken out of the "water" so the fish and other creatures can then live happily in the water.
8. Have the child set the water toys next to the water, as you explain how we always need to be careful that we do not leave our toys in the water.

Children's Books

Lake and Pond by
April Pulley Sayre
Living Near a River by
Allan Fowler
*What Lives in Streams
and Rivers?* by
Oona Gaarder-Juntti

ASSESSMENT

Consider the following:
- Can the children identify items that do not belong in the water?
- Do the children understand the importance of keeping water clean?

Mary J. Murray, Mazomanie, WI

Greenhouse Growth

4+

LEARNING OBJECTIVES

The children will:
1. Compare growth of plants in greenhouses to growth of uncovered seeds.
2. Compare water use by both groups of plants.
3. Begin to consider the effects of human actions on the environment.

Materials

pots
potting soil
seeds
clear plastic bags
   big enough to
   cover plants and
   allow room for
   growth
sticks to support
   the tops of each
   bag

VOCABULARY

air	greenhouse	moisten	temperature
compare	grow	soil	water
experiment	growth		

PREPARATION

● Fill pots with soil and plant seeds in the soil.

WHAT TO DO

1. Engage the children in a conversation about greenhouses. Explain that greenhouses are supposed to help plants grow.
2. Show the children the bags and help the children plant seeds in them. Make sure all plants have water. Explain how these bags are like greenhouses.
3. Over the next few days, watch for signs of plant growth. Make a note of whether plants with greenhouses sprout first. Consider whether they use more water. Note other effects, including moss growth or lack of flies. Discuss why these effects may occur.
4. Before removing the greenhouses, allow the children to slip a hand or finger inside. Talk with the children about moisture and temperature. Remove the greenhouses when the plants are close to the top.
5. Ask the children what would happen to the plant if we didn't include water, changed the air inside to something else, removed the air before closing the bags, or left garbage in the greenhouse.

Children's Books

Abuelito's Greenhouse by Susan Ring
Mr. Percy's Magic Greenhouse by Anthea Kemp
Out and About at the Greenhouse by Bitsy Kemper

ASSESSMENT

Consider the following:
● Do the children notice the effects of the greenhouses on plant growth?
● Do the children see the condensation and judge the water use?
● Do the children begin to consider the effects of human actions on the environment?

Debbie Vilardi, Commack, NY

Living Things

4

LEARNING OBJECTIVES

The children will:
1. Classify objects that are alive and not alive.
2. Recognize that things are alive.

Materials

picture of the
   teacher as a child
pictures of the
   children
pictures of living
   and nonliving
   things
large sheets of
   paper (1 per
   child)
glue

VOCABULARY

alive	grow	nonliving	sort
classify	living	object	

PREPARATION

* Ahead of time, ask the children to bring in a picture of themselves.
* Fold paper in half and label one side "living" and the other side "not living."

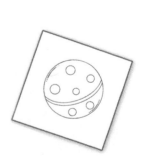

WHAT TO DO

1. Show the picture of yourself and explain that it is you when you were younger.
2. Tell the children how old you were then and ask them what differences they notice.
3. Ask the children if they will grow too and if their picture will grow. Why not? List their answers on the board. Focus on the concept of living. Discuss what else lives.
4. Give each child a picture of a living or nonliving thing. Have the children sort their picture into a "living" or "not living" group one at a time, and write their answers on the board. The rest of the children can help decide if they are correct.
5. Give each child a packet of new pictures and a sheet to classify them on. Have them glue the pictures on the correct half of the paper.

TEACHER-TO-TEACHER TIP

* Pictures of the children could be included in the packets.

ASSESSMENT

Consider the following:
* Are the children able to classify the objects correctly?
* Are the children able to recognize what is alive?

Debbie Vilardi, Commack, NY

Children's Books

I Am a Living Thing by
   Bobbie Kalman
Living and Nonliving by
   Angela Royston
What's Alive? by
   Kathleen Weidner
   Zoehfeld

Ocean Days

Materials

globe or world map
sand bucket
beanbag ocean and
    land animals
blue blanket
sunglasses

LEARNING OBJECTIVES

The children will:
1. Learn about the ocean.
2. Reproduce, extend, and create patterns.
3. Improve their oral language skills.

VOCABULARY

animal	fish	land	ocean
crab	globe	map	

WHAT TO DO

1. Display a globe or world map. Draw the children's attention to the large bodies of water. Ask the children if they know what they are called. Explain that they are oceans.
2. Set out a sand bucket filled with beanbag ocean animals and land animals, and show each animal to the children, asking the children to clap if the animal belongs in the ocean, and to sit quietly if the animal lives on the land.
3. After going through the animals, place a blue blanket in the center of the circle. Put an animal behind each child's back as they sit in a circle. Ask the children not to look at their animals until you call their names.
4. Teach the children the following ocean chant, inviting them to bring their animals, one by one, and say the animals' names in the appropriate places:

Big Blue Ocean by Mary J. Murray
Big blue ocean, filled with life,
There's so much to learn.
Show us what you have, ____ (child's name)
Now it's your turn.
I have a ____. (children take turns saying the names of their animals)

ASSESSMENT

Consider the following:
- Can the children differentiate between objects that do and do not belong in the ocean?
- Display an assortment of objects that do and do not belong in the ocean. Ask a child to pick up the objects that "don't belong" and put them in a sand pail.

Children's Books

Beaches by
Emma Bernay
*Do You Know About
Life in the Sea?* by
Philip Steele
*The Ocean Alphabet
Book* by Jerry Pallotta

Mary J. Murray, Mazomanie, WI

Shrinking Polar Ice

4+

LEARNING OBJECTIVES

The children will:
1. Investigate how shrinking polar ice affects polar creatures.
2. Learn why a solid turns into a liquid.

Materials

scissors (adult use only)
large white paper
masking tape
ice cubes
sandwich bags (1 per child and teacher)
picture of polar bear
The Three Snow Bears by Jan Brett
music

VOCABULARY

cold	ice	liquid	polar bear
freeze	ice cap	melt	solid
hard	ice floe		

PREPARATION
- Cut enough paper "ice floes" for each child to stand on; tape them to the floor.

WHAT TO DO
1. Give each child an ice cube in a closed sandwich bag. Have them describe the ice (white or clear, cold, hard).
2. Show the polar bear picture to the children. Compare it to the ice cube (color, needs cold places to survive).
3. Ask what is happening to their ice cube, and explain that polar ice caps are enormous sheets of ice, so when the water gets warmer, pieces break off into ice floes that float away.
4. Read *The Three Snow Bears* by Jan Brett. Who had a problem with ice floes? Who needs cold weather?
5. Play musical ice floes using musical chairs rules and the ice floes taped to the floor. Take away floes when the music stops until one child remains on a floe.
6. Ask the children how they felt when their ice floe disappeared, and how they think polar bears feel if their ice melts.

TEACHER-TO-TEACHER TIP
- Put your ice cube near a heat source to make the melting more visible. Ask the children why yours melted more than theirs did.

ASSESSMENT
Consider the following:
- Can the children describe what has happened to the ice?
- Do the children make a connection between what happened to the ice cube and what is happening to the polar ice caps?

Children's Books

Our Earth by Anne Rockwell
We Share One World by Jane E. Hoffelt
Where the Forest Meets the Sea by Jeannie Baker

Terry Callahan, Easton, MD

Science Slides

4+

LEARNING OBJECTIVES

The children will:

1. Learn about how scientists sort and classify objects in nature.
2. Learn how to describe objects from nature.

Materials

plastic sleeves
   (1 for each child)
nature items
tape
magnifying glass

VOCABULARY

classify	explore	magnify
collect	investigate	slide
describe	nature	sort

PREPARATION

- Purchase a plastic sleeve for each child. The best sleeves to use are those used for collecting baseball cards (heavy, plastic 3" × 4" sleeves with one of the four sides open).
- Send home the plastic sleeves with a note for parents. For example:

Dear parents and family members,

Please help your child find a nature item (leaf, stalk of grass, flower, and so on) and put it in this sleeve to make a "slide." Have your child bring it back to school. I will put these items in our science center for the children to examine and explore.

Thank you,

- When the children return with the "slides," write each child's name on the slide. Use tape to secure the open end closed so the children cannot remove the item.

WHAT TO DO

1. Ask the children to tell the class about their slides. Encourage them to talk about where and how they collected their items.
2. Put different slides in the science center throughout the year. Encourage the children to explore the items with a magnifying glass. They get especially excited because they each have contributed to this collection.

ASSESSMENT

Consider the following:

- Do the children have a particular interest in specific slides?
- What does each child bring in? What do they say about the items?

Children's Books

Are Trees Alive? by Debbie S. Miller
The Everything Kids Environment Book by Sheri Amsel
We Share One World by Jane E. Hoffelt

Gail Morris, Kemah, TX

Thank a Tree

4+

LEARNING OBJECTIVES

The children will:
1. Name at least two of the many things we get from trees.
2. Develop fine motor skills and the ability to print alphabet letters.

apple
piece of writing
    paper
wooden classroom
    chair
pencil
blank "thank-you"
    cards or blank
    pieces of paper
    cut to 5" × 7"
pencils, colored
    pencils, crayons,
    and markers

VOCABULARY

apple	message	pecans	thank-you note
bananas	paper	pencil	tree
maple syrup	pears	shade	wooden

WHAT TO DO

1. Show the children an apple, a piece of writing paper, a wooden classroom chair, and a pencil. Ask them what those things have in common. Lead them to the conclusion that all four came from trees.
2. Ask the children what other things we get from trees or ask them to name some things that trees do for us (maple syrup, pears, pecans, and bananas all come from trees; trees provide shade for us on hot summer days).
3. Ask the children to write a thank-you note to the trees on the playground or around your center. Help the children compose and print a simple message using a variety of writing instruments on the note paper.
4. Take your notes outside and place them at the foot of the trees for which they are intended (weighted with rocks to protect them from the wind) or hang the note on a branch by spearing the paper on a small twig.
   Note: After a day or two, thank the tree one more time by recycling the note.

ASSESSMENT

Consider the following:
- Are the children able to describe the trees and say what the trees do for them?
- While helping children print their thank-you cards to the trees, observe whether anyone attempts to sound out the words.

Virginia Jean Herrod, Columbia, SC

Children's Books

The Giving Tree by
    Shel Silverstein
A Tree Is Nice by
    Janice May Udry
*Where the Forest Meets
    the Sea* by
    Jeannie Baker

Tree Hugger

4+

LEARNING OBJECTIVES

The children will:

1. Develop an appreciation for trees and their respective sizes.
2. Learn the names of the different parts of trees.

Materials

posters and books
  detailing tree
  parts
whiteboard or
  poster

VOCABULARY

bark	leaves	tall	tree
branch	roots	thick	trunk
buds	short	thin	twig

WHAT TO DO

1. Show the children a picture of a tree and have them describe what they see. Write their words on a whiteboard or poster. Does anyone have a tree in their yard at home? How about a favorite tree?
2. Go through a tree diagram with them, pointing out the parts and sketching a larger tree on the board. Label the parts. Consider having the children draw tree pictures.
3. Show various pictures of trees and talk with the children about how different trees can be. Explain that trees can be tall or short, thick or thin. Discuss these qualities and say that the class will soon be going outside to make friends with the trees!
4. Take the children outside and have them gather around a tree. Ask the children to name the parts of the tree; discuss the bark, leaves, trunk, and branches, as well as the roots and other hidden parts. Ask a child to try and hug the tree. Can the child join his hands together around it? Is this tree *thick* or *thin*? If another child joins hands with the first, can the two reach their arms all the way around the tree? Let the children explore the area and find the thickest, thinnest, tallest, and shortest trees.

ASSESSMENT

Consider the following:

- Can the children name the various parts of a tree?
- Can the children describe the characteristics of various trees?

Patrick Mitchell, Yagoto, Nagoya, Japan

Children's Books

Tell Me, Tree: All About Trees for Kids by Gail Gibbons
A Tree in a Forest by Jan Thornhill
A Tree Is Nice by Janice May Udry

Trees

4+

LEARNING OBJECTIVES

The children will:
1. Develop respect for our environment.
2. Learn about trees and why they are important.
3. Learn how to plant a tree.

Materials

seedling tree
large shovel
small shovels for
    the children
new soil (if needed)

VOCABULARY

air	outside	shovel	tree
bird	plant	soil	water
dig	shade	sun	

PREPARATION

● Have an approved spot in the yard or garden to plant a tree. Make sure the soil is ready for planting and that it will be easy to use a shovel in that area. Dig as needed.

WHAT TO DO

1. Explain that today the children will plant a tree.
2. Talk with the children first. Do they know why trees are important? (They help purify the air, provide homes for birds and other creatures, provide shade to keep animals and people cool, prevent erosion, and act as windbreaks.)
3. Ask the children to follow you outside to the designated tree-planting site. Each child participates in shoveling, setting in new soil, helping put the tree in the ground, or watering.

TEACHER-TO-TEACHER TIP

● Some children are stronger than others, but be sure everyone participates in at least one of the activities.

ASSESSMENT

Consider the following:
● Can the children tell you why trees are important?
● Can the children describe how to plant a tree?

Children's Books

Curious George Plants a Tree by H. A. Rey
The Life Cycle of a Tree by Bobbie Kalman
A Tree Is a Plant by Clyde Robert Bulla

Shirley Anne Ramaley, Sun City, AZ

Trees and Leaves

4+

LEARNING OBJECTIVES

The children will:
1. Become familiar with the parts of a tree.
2. Learn about how animals and people need trees.
3. Gather information using sense of touch, smell, and sight.

Materials

pictures of trees
leaves
construction paper
crayons

VOCABULARY

animals	branch	root	trunk
bark	leaf	tree	wood

WHAT TO DO

1. Show the children pictures of trees and engage them in a discussion about trees. Discuss how animals live in trees, how we eat food from trees, and how we harvest trees for wood.
2. Point out the parts of a tree: trunk, leaves, branches, bark, roots, and so on.
3. Take the children on a walk to visit a live tree. Ask them to identify the parts of the tree. Look for animals in and around the tree.
4. Encourage them to describe what the tree looks, smells, and feels like.
5. Ask the children what that spot would be like without the tree.
6. Back in the classroom, set out the various leaves and invite the children to draw outlines of them on paper, make leaf rubbings, or to try and draw portraits of the leaves.

ASSESSMENT

Consider the following:
- Can the children look at a picture of a tree and identify the leaves and the trunk?
- Gather the children around a picture of a tree and ask them to point out the trunk, branches, leaves, and any other visible parts of the tree.

Children's Books

Are Trees Alive? by Debbie S. Miller
The Great Kapok Tree by Lynne Cherry
A Tree Is Nice by Janice May Udry

Cassandra Reigel Whetstone, Folsom, CA

How to Appreciate Nature **5+**

LEARNING OBJECTIVES

The children will:
1. Learn how to appreciate nature.
2. Learn to care for the world around them.
3. Develop their capacity to pay attention.

Materials

school yard or an area park with trees, plants, and flowers
Earth by Penelope York
S Is for Save the Planet: A How-to-Be Green Alphabet by Brad Herzog
Sesame Street Let's Help the Earth by Reader's Digest

Children's Books

1000 Facts on Planet Earth by John Farndon
Eye Wonder: Earth by D.K. Publishing
Hello Sun! by Hans Wilhelm

VOCABULARY

bark	grass	nature	shade of color
flower	hue	plant	tree

WHAT TO DO

1. Take the children on a walk outside your school or in a nearby park. Point out the various colors that you encounter during the walk. Note the shades of greens in trees, plants, and grass.
2. Observe the various shades of brown in the different tree barks, the blue sky and white clouds. Discuss the bright colors and soft pastel hues of the different flowers. When you return to the classroom, show the vibrant color illustrations of our Earth in the book *Earth* by Penelope York.
3. Point out the many different colors across the Earth's landscape.
4. As the week progresses, read several poems each day in *S Is for Save the Planet: A How-to-Be Green Alphabet* by Brad Herzog and show the illustrations.

5. Read the book *Sesame Street Let's Help the Earth*, and note that Elmo is helping our Earth by recycling, saving water, turning off lights, and planting trees and flowers. Share each of these illustrations.

ASSESSMENT

Consider the following:
- Are the children able to notice the colors in nature?
- Are the children willing to help preserve the beauty of our Earth?

Annie Laura Smith, Huntsville, AL

Sensational Sun

5+

LEARNING OBJECTIVES

The children will:
1. Learn that the Earth moves around the sun.
2. Learn that the Earth rotates on its axis once a day.
3. Develop their large motor skills.

Materials

yellow balloon
globe
blue tissue paper

VOCABULARY

axis	Earth	night	rotate
day	globe	rain	sun

WHAT TO DO

1. Hold up a yellow balloon high above a globe on a table.
2. Show the children how day and night arrive. Remind the children that the sun does not go away and come back; the Earth simply spins around on its axis so that the sun shines on parts of the Earth at different times.
3. Tell the children that it takes 24 hours for the Earth to spin itself around.
4. Tell the children to stand in a large circle on the floor. Place "raindrops" (blue tissue paper balls) around the outside of the area.
5. With your hands, tap the yellow balloon high into the air and invite two children to keep tapping the "sun" so that it stays up in the sky. Make sure to let all the children get a turn tapping the balloon.
6. Each time a child taps the balloon, have the children say "sunny day" in unison.
7. Every so often, announce a "rainy day" and hold on to the sun. Invite the children to pick up blue raindrops, toss them up into the air, and let them land on the ground.

ASSESSMENT

Consider the following:
- Do the children understand that the Earth rotates on its axis?
- Can the children say how long it takes for the Earth to rotate on its axis, and how long it takes to travel around the sun?

Mary J. Murray, Mazomanie, WI

Children's Books

Hello Sun! by
Hans Wilhelm
*The Sun Is My Favorite
Star* by Frank Asch
Sunshine by Gail
Saunders-Smith

Twitter and Warble

5+

LEARNING OBJECTIVES

The children will:
1. Recognize selected bird calls.
2. Practice listening skills in preparation for sounding out words in reading.
3. Learn the importance of birds in nature.

Materials

pictures of local birds
recording of calls and songs of local birds (borrow from library)
cardboard or poster board
large permanent markers

VOCABULARY

beak	nature	pollination	song
bird	pesticide	population	vermin
herbicide	poison	reforest	

PREPARATION

- Select five or more local birds for the children to learn about. Be sure the calls and songs are distinctive enough for the children to easily recognize.
- Write the bird names on cardboard or poster board in capital letters, using large permanent markers.
- Display bird pictures with names underneath. Have a CD or other recording of each bird's call or song.

WHAT TO DO

1. Teach the children the importance of birds. Birds control insect and vermin population; reforest trees and fruit plants by dropping seeds; pollinate plants (hummingbirds); and so on.
2. Discuss how the overuse of herbicides and pesticides poisons and sickens birds.
3. Teach the children how to identify selected birds by sight and sound.
4. Play selected bird calls and songs, holding up the appropriate picture and bird name.
5. After a few days, the children should be starting to differentiate between the bird calls and songs, matching the correct bird and even the name. Discretionary listening is essential for prereading skills, to hear the difference between a "b" and a "d," for example. This is one way to make it both interesting and educational.

ASSESSMENT

Consider the following:
- Do the children show an interest in listening to birds outdoors?
- Can the children correctly match bird pictures to bird calls and songs?

Children's Books

The Earth and I by Frank Asch
The Giving Tree by Shel Silverstein
What's a Jaybird to Do? by Cat Sauer

Kay Flowers, Summerfield, OH

Water Conservation

5+

LEARNING OBJECTIVES

The children will:
1. Learn about water conservation.
2. Develop respect for the environment.
3. Increase vocabulary and language skills.
4. Increase prewriting skills.
5. Practice writing the letters that make the words "water conservation."

Materials

writing paper
art paper
pencils
colored pencils or
   crayons

VOCABULARY

conservation	ecology	freshwater	salt water
drip	environment	lake	well
Earth	faucet	river	

PREPARATION
● Place the materials on the children's tables.

WHAT TO DO

1. Discuss water, how it is important, and how we can all conserve it.
2. Do the children have any ideas for how to conserve water? Encourage them to talk about their ideas.
3. Talk about turning off water when it's not being used, not letting water run when we brush our teeth, and making sure the faucet is completely off so it doesn't drip.
4. Explain where drinking water comes from (lakes, rivers, or wells).
5. Discuss important facts about water: It is a limited resource. There is only so much of it. People get sick if they don't have enough water or if their water is dirty.
6. We can help keep water clean by not throwing trash into any water.
7. Have the children practice writing the letters for the words "water conservation." If they want, they can draw and color a picture with water in it, above the words. Sign their names and post this for all to see.

Children's Books

Water by Trevor Day
The Water Cycle by Trudi Strain Trueit
Water Power by Christine Petersen

ASSESSMENT
Consider the following:
● Do the children know where water comes from?
● What are the children's ideas about conserving water?
● Ask the children why water is important.

Shirley Anne Ramaley, Sun City, AZ

Whales in the Ocean

5+

LEARNING OBJECTIVES

The children will:
1. Learn that whales live in the ocean.
2. Discuss ways to care for the ocean and the whales that live in the ocean.

Materials

pictures of various
whales
cards with whale
names on them

VOCABULARY

beluga whale	describe	killer whale	orca whale
blue whale	discuss	ocean	

WHAT TO DO

1. Engage the children in a discussion about the different creatures that live in the ocean. Explain that it is important to keep the ocean clean so that these creatures can survive and thrive.
2. Ask the children about whales. Can they describe whales? Do they know that there are a variety of different kinds of whales? Ask the children what they can do to help keep the ocean clean for the whales.
3. Display various pictures of whales. Show the children the cards with the names of the various whales written on them.
4. Go through the names of the whales with the children. Then, help the children learn the names of each whale and then teach someone else about the different types of whales in the ocean.
5. Encourage the children to discuss together ways that they can help keep the ocean clean so that whales can thrive.

Children's Books

Beaches by
Emma Bernay
*Do You Know About
Life in the Sea?* by
Philip Steele
*The Ocean Alphabet
Book* by Jerry Pallotta

ASSESSMENT

Consider the following:
- Can the children name various whales?
- Do the children understand that it is important to care for the ocean so that whales can live safely?

Mary J. Murray, Mazomanie, WI

Beautiful Beaches

4+

LEARNING OBJECTIVES

The children will:
1. Complete puzzles.
2. Develop visual discrimination skills.
3. Develop appreciation for our beaches.

Materials

pictures of coastal
   and beach
   scenes
laminator
scissors (adult use
   only)
resealable plastic
   bags

VOCABULARY

beach	ocean	puzzle	sea
jigsaw	protect	sand	

PREPARATION

- Collect pictures of coastal and beach scenes. Old calendars work well.
- Laminate each picture, and then cut it into pieces to create a simple jigsaw puzzle.
- Place each set of puzzle pieces in a resealable plastic bag.

WHAT TO DO

1. Ask how many of the children have been to the beach. What is their favorite thing about the beach? What do they like to do there? Explain that it's important to protect our beaches so that we can enjoy them for years to come.
2. Tell the children that they will be putting together jigsaw puzzles of pictures of beaches.
3. Give each child a set of puzzle pieces and have her complete the puzzle.
4. If some children finish quickly, they can trade puzzles with one another.

POEM

The Beach by Laura Wynkoop
I love to travel to the beach.
I love to watch the sea.
The sand is warm, the water's cool.
It's just the place for me!

ASSESSMENT

Consider the following:
- Are the children able to complete one or more puzzles?
- Can the children tell you what they like about the beach?

Children's Books

At the Beach by
Anne Rockwell
*Curious George Goes to
the Beach* by H. A. Rey
Going to the Beach by
Jo S. Kittinger
Sea, Sand, Me! by
Patricia Hubbell

Laura Wynkoop, San Dimas, CA

"Caring for Our Earth" Puzzle

4+

LEARNING OBJECTIVES

The children will:
1. Increase their visual perceptual skills.
2. Put a puzzle together.
3. Develop their small motor skills.

Materials

picture of two
  hands holding
  the Earth
tagboard
child-safe scissors
glue stick
9" × 12" manila
  envelope
Velcro

VOCABULARY

care   Earth   puzzle

WHAT TO DO

1. Locate a picture approximately 6" × 6" of two hands holding the Earth (the Internet is a good source). Copy it onto tagboard, and make one for each child.
2. Help the children cut out six or more squares from the picture like windows, leaving part of the picture intact surrounding each square cutout. The squares will be the puzzle pieces.
3. Have the children glue the remaining picture, with the squares removed, to the front of a 9" × 12" envelope.
4. Attach Velcro pieces to the back of each puzzle piece and to each open square on the picture on the envelope.
5. Have the children attach the pieces to the envelope to complete the puzzle. Store the pieces in the envelope when not in use.

TEACHER-TO-TEACHER TIP
- To find an appropriate picture on the Internet for this activity, search for "happy Earth."

ASSESSMENT
Consider the following:
- What do the children think that the image of hands holding the Earth means?
- How well do the children use the scissors and other items? Do they need help?

Jackie Wright, Enid, OK

Children's Books

The Earth and I by Frank Asch
The Great Trash Bash by Loreen Leedy
Grover's 10 Terrific Ways to Help Our Wonderful World by Anna Ross
Johnny and the Old Oak Tree by Rachel Peterpaul Paulson

Garden Party

3+

LEARNING OBJECTIVES

The children will:
1. Celebrate their class garden.
2. Share what they have grown and learned with family and friends.

Materials

blankets
plates
cups
napkins
food and drinks

VOCABULARY

celebrate	flowers	grow	plants
chart	garden	picnic	welcome

PREPARATION

- This activity is a way to include the children's families in the classroom's experience of growing a garden.
- Send invitations home for a garden party.
- Pick and wash food grown in your class garden. If it is a flower garden, discuss picking flowers for bouquets with the class. The children may prefer to have the flowers remain in the garden.
- Prepare displays of plant growth charts and other parts of the children's work.

WHAT TO DO

1. Welcome guests. Have each family spread out a picnic blanket to sit on.
2. Let the children show the garden to their families and describe the work they did in the garden.
3. Display the books about gardening that you read to the children, and share the garden-related poems and fingerplays with the children's families.
4. Eat the foods you have grown in the class garden. Consider adding traditional garden party foods such as finger sandwiches and lemonade.

TEACHER-TO-TEACHER TIP

- Plan a rain date. Remember that some flowers are also edible. Since you've been learning about garbage, consider reducing it by using dishes instead of paper goods.

ASSESSMENT

Consider the following:
- Do the children explain the garden to their family members?
- Do the children help to pick the food from the garden?

Children's Books

Compost Critters by Bianca Lavies
Growing Vegetable Soup by Lois Ehlert
Zinnia's Flower Garden by Monica Wellington

Debbie Vilardi, Commack, NY

Sun Snack

4+

LEARNING OBJECTIVES

The children will:

1. Learn that the sun helps food to grow.
2. Enjoy a healthy snack.

Materials

pineapple
bananas
strips of yellow
    pepper
paper plates

VOCABULARY

banana	edible	important	snack
circle	flower	pineapple	sun
Earth	grow	ring	sunbeams

WHAT TO DO

1. Talk with the children about the importance of the sun.
2. Explain how it helps everything to grow, from trees to flowers to the food they eat. Talk about how the sun gives off sunbeams that travel through space, and help all things in nature to grow. Point out that without the sun, there would be nothing to eat.
3. Explain that for snack the children will be making edible suns.
4. Give each child a pineapple ring or a circular slice of banana in its peel, and several thin strips of yellow pepper.
5. Ask the children to describe the sun. Ask them to talk about how these foods resemble the sun.
6. Invite the children to create suns on their plates, using the bananas or pineapples as the suns, and the pepper strips as sunrays.
7. Encourage the children to eat their suns, piece by piece.

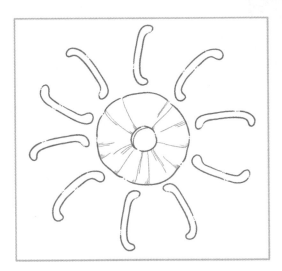

ASSESSMENT

Consider the following:

- Ask the children what the sun does to help food grow?
- Can the children identify the color of the sun?

Children's Books

Hello Sun! by Hans Wilhelm
The Sun Is My Favorite Star by Frank Asch
Sunshine by Gail Saunders-Smith

Mary J. Murray, Mazomanie, WI

I Like the Ocean

3+

LEARNING OBJECTIVES

The children will:
1. Memorize a short rhyme.
2. Learn to say the names of various sea creatures.

Materials

beanbag

VOCABULARY

beanbag	fish	octopus	shark
crab	lobster	sea	whale
creature	ocean		

WHAT TO DO

1. Engage the children in a discussion about the ocean. Ask the children to name various creatures that live in the sea.
2. Talk with the children about how important it is to care for the ocean, so the creatures in the ocean can thrive.
3. Teach the children the following original rhyme:

I Like the Ocean by Mary J. Murray
I like the ocean; I help keep it big and blue.
I like the ocean, how about you?

4. Each time the children chant the word "you," the child holding the beanbag tosses it to a different child.
5. The child who catches the beanbag responds by naming a sea creature.

ASSESSMENT

Consider the following:
- Can the children recite the poem? How easily do they learn the words?
- Can the children name a sea creature when they catch the beanbag?

Mary J. Murray, Mazomanie, WI

Children's Books

Going to the Beach by Jo S. Kittinger
The Ocean Alphabet Book by Jerry Pallotta
Sea, Sand, Me! by Patricia Hubbell

Recycle and Save the Earth

3+

LEARNING OBJECTIVES

The children will:
1. Learn the meaning of recycling.
2. Reinforce caring for the world.
3. Improve their language skills.

Materials

VOCABULARY

conserve	landfill	reuse	song
Earth	recycle	sing	trash

WHAT TO DO

1. Talk to the children about what recycling means. Tell them how good things can be made from what we might otherwise put into the trash and landfill sites.
2. Teach them the following recycling song. **Note:** Sing the word "once" as though it had two syllables.

   Recycle and Save the Earth by Anne Adeney
   (Tune: "Frère Jacques")
   Let's recycle, let's recycle!
   You and me, you and me!
   Use stuff more than once, use stuff more than once!
   Save the Earth, save the Earth!

3. Sing this song whenever appropriate. Encourage the children to think of times when it would be appropriate to sing the song.

ASSESSMENT

Consider the following:
- Can the children tell you what "recycling" means?
- Can the children name something used more than once.

Anne Adeney, Plymouth, United Kingdom

Children's Books

Michael Recycle by Ellie Bethel
The Three Rs: Reuse, Reduce, Recycle by Nuria Roca
Why Should I Recycle? by Jen Green

Taking Care of My Little Tree 3+

LEARNING OBJECTIVES

The children will:
1. Develop their memorization skills.
2. Learn about taking care of trees.

Materials

VOCABULARY

bird	fruit	shade	tree	weeds
care	nest	squirrel	watering	wood

WHAT TO DO

1. Recite the following rhyme and do the actions with the children:

   Taking Care of My Little Tree by Ingelore Mix
   In my garden stands a little tree (rest elbow on tabletop with fingers straight up
       not spread apart)
   Tweedledum and Tweedledee,
   I take good care of my little tree.
   Tweedledum and Tweedledee,
   I pull out weeds around the tree. (use other hand to pretend to pull weeds)
   Tweedledum and Tweedledee,
   I always water my little tree. (use other hand to pretend to water by wiggling fingers)
   Tweedledum and Tweedledee,
   It grows and grows my little tree. (stretch arm up and spread fingers apart)
   Tweedledum and Tweedledee,
   Now birds and squirrels nest in my tree. (cup both hands like a nest)
   Tweedledum and Tweedledee,
   I'm glad I took care of my tree.
   Tweedledum and Tweedledee.

2. Talk with the children about different trees and their leaves. Ask the children if they can name other things people get from trees, such as wood, fruits, shade, and so on.

3. Find items in the classroom that are made from wood. Follow up with a walk outside.

ASSESSMENT

Consider the following:
- Can the children recite ways to care for a tree, from the lyrics of the fingerplay?
- Can the children name things that people get from trees?

> Ingelore Mix, Gainesville, VA

Children's Books

The Giving Tree by Shel Silverstein
Johnny and the Old Oak Tree by Rachel Peterpaul Paulson
The Lorax by Dr. Seuss

E-A-R-T-H

LEARNING OBJECTIVES

The children will:
1. Learn to spell "Earth."
2. Practice left-to-right reading skills.

Materials

card stock or
   construction
   paper
child-safe scissors
glue stick
gummy adhesive
laminator (optional)
binding machine
   (optional)

VOCABULARY

Earth   missing

PREPARATION

- Copy the words of the song "E-A-R-T-H" onto a large sheet of construction paper.
- From paper, cut out six pages the same length of the backboard but only ⅓ to ½ as tall, so they will not cover the words above them.
- Cut out five copies of each of the letters E, A, R, T, and H. Glue each set to one of the pages, leaving E off the first page, A off the second, R off the third, and so on. Leave space for the missing letter.
- Bind the pages in order to a piece of cardstock so that you can flip them down as you go through the song.
- Make a set of manipulative letters that spell out "Earth."

WHAT TO DO

1. Sing the following song and ask one child at a time to find the missing letter and place it on the page using gummy adhesive:

E-A-R-T-H by Jackie Wright
(Tune: "Bingo")
We take care of our planet
And Earth is its name-o.
Please help me spell its name.
Please help me spell its name.
Please help me spell its name.
Earth is its name-o.

Children's Books

Our Earth by
Anne Rockwell
*Recycle! A Handbook
for Kids* by
Gail Gibbons
Why Should I Recycle?
by Jen Green

ASSESSMENT

Consider the following:
- Do the children display an interest in the activity?
- Are the children able to find the correct letter and place it where it should go?

Jackie Wright , Enid, OK

I'm the Planet Earth

4+

LEARNING OBJECTIVES

The children will:

1. Learn about the Earth as seen from space.
2. Develop their memorization skills.

Materials

VOCABULARY

blue	green	river	town
brown	marvelous	space	view
Earth	planet	tree	white

WHAT TO DO

1. Teach the children the following song:

I'm the Planet Earth by Virginia Jean Herrod
(Tune: "I'm a Little Teapot")
I'm the planet Earth,
Green, blue, brown, and white.
Seen from space
I'm a marvelous sight.

You can't see my trees,
My rivers or my towns.
From space all you see
Is green, blue, white, and brown.

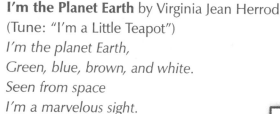

ASSESSMENT

Consider the following:

● Do the children learn the words to the song?
● Can the children name the colors mentioned in the song?

Virginia Jean Herrod, Columbia, SC

Children's Books

Big Earth, Little Me
by Thom Wiley
How We Learned the
Earth Is Round
by Patricia Lauber
I Love Our Earth
by Bill Martin Jr. and
Michael Sampson
The Librarian Who
Measured the Earth
by Kathryn Lasky and
Kevin Hawkes
Planet Earth/Inside Out
by Gail Gibbons
You're Aboard
Spaceship Earth
by Patricia Lauber

The More We Love Our Earth

LEARNING OBJECTIVES

The children will:
1. Sing about loving the Earth.
2. Develop their memory skills.

Materials

VOCABULARY

bottle	happy	newspaper	recycle	reuse
Earth	love	plastic	reduce	sprinkler

WHAT TO DO

1. Teach the children the following song:

The More We Love Our Earth by Virginia Jean Herrod
(Tune: "The More We Get Together")

The more we love our Earth,
Our Earth, our Earth,
The more we love our Earth
The happier we'll be.
For we can recycle,
Reuse, and reduce.
The more we love our Earth
The happier we'll be.

The more we love our Earth,
Our Earth, our Earth.
The more we love our Earth
The happier we'll be.

Reduce your use of water
Don't run those sprinklers.
The more we love our Earth
The happier we'll be.

Recycle your plastic bottles.
They make great carpets.
The more we love our Earth
The happier we'll be.

Reuse those old newspapers.
They're great for art projects.
The more we love our Earth
The happier we'll be.

ASSESSMENT

Consider the following:
- Do the children learn the words to the song?
- Do the children understand the importance of recycling?

Virginia Jean Herrod, Columbia, SC

Children's Books

Metal by Alexandra Fix
Paper by Alexandra Fix
Reduce, Reuse, Recycle Plastic by Alexandra Fix
Stuff! Reduce, Reuse, Recycle by Steven Kroll

Our Sun

4+

LEARNING OBJECTIVES

The children will:
1. Learn that the sun is a burning hot ball of gases and flames.
2. Understand that the sun warms the Earth.
3. Learn that the sun helps keep people, animals, and plants alive and growing.
4. Differentiate between the sun, the moon, and the Earth.

Materials

pictures of the sun, moon, and Earth

VOCABULARY

Earth	hot	planet	sun
gas	light	plant	tree
grow	moon	shine	
heat	night	space	

WHAT TO DO

1. Engage the children in a discussion about the sun. Explain that the sun is very far off in space, but that it is so hot we feel its heat, and it helps everything on Earth to grow.
2. Show the children the pictures of the sun, and encourage them to describe what they see. **Safety Note:** Remind the children never to look directly into the sun.
3. Teach the children the following fingerplay and actions:

Our Sun by Mary J. Murray
The sun shines and warms the Earth. (stand with arms in circle above head)
It also gives us light. (place hand over eyebrow to block sun)
It causes plants and trees to grow. (arms grow upward like a plant)
And shines on the moon at night. (head on hands—sleeping motion)

ASSESSMENT

Consider the following:
- Display pictures of the sun, the moon, and the Earth. Can the children name and differentiate between the three?
- Do the children understand that the Earth needs the sun?

Mary J. Murray, Mazomanie, WI

Children's Books

Hello Sun!
by Hans Wilhelm
The Sun Is My Favorite Star by Frank Asch
Sunshine by Gail Saunders-Smith

Pick It Up!

4+

LEARNING OBJECTIVES

The children will:
1. Learn about littering.
2. Develop oral language skills.
3. Develop their sense of rhythm.

Materials

VOCABULARY

clean	garbage	litter	plants
environment	green	planet	

WHAT TO DO

1. Teach the children the following song:

   Pick It Up by Laura Wynkoop
   (Tune: "If You're Happy And You Know It")
   If you find a bit of garbage, pick it up.
   If you find a bit of garbage, pick it up.
   You can make our planet cleaner,
   And our plants a little greener,
   If you find a bit of garbage, pick it up.

2. Tell the children it helps the
   environment to pick up litter.
   Remind them to always wash
   their hands after picking up litter.

ASSESSMENT

Consider the following:
- Do the children learn to sing
  the song?
- Ask the children what they should do
  when they see garbage on the ground.

Laura Wynkoop, San Dimas, CA

Children's Books

Earth Smart by
Leslie Garrett
Lady Lulu Liked to Litter
by Nancy Loewen
*Why Does Litter Cause
Problems?* by
Isaac Asimov

The Recycling Song

Materials

Children's Books

Let's Recycle!
by Anne L. Mackenzie
Recycle Every Day!
by Nancy Elizabeth
Wallace
*We Are Extremely Very
Good Recyclers*
by Lauren Child
Why Should I Recycle?
by Jen Green

LEARNING OBJECTIVES

The children will:
1. Learn a song about recycling.
2. Reinforce the types of items that can be recycled.

VOCABULARY

aluminum	Earth	plastic
bottle	green	recycling
can	newspaper	recycling bin
clean	paper	tin

PREPARATION

● Consider creating gestures that go with the words of the song.

WHAT TO DO

1. Teach the children "The Recycling Song" by repeating it several times:

The Recycling Song by Christina Chilcote
(Tune: "Twinkle, Twinkle, Little Star")
*We will help keep our Earth green.
We will help keep our Earth clean.
Paper, plastic, cans of tin,
Toss them in the recycling bin.
Plastic bottles, newspaper too,
Recycling's good for the Earth and you.*

2. Have the children join you in singing the
song. Include appropriate gestures, if you wish. Talk
about things that are recyclable.

ASSESSMENT

Consider the following:
● Can each of the children sing the song along with the rest of the class?
● Can the children identify different items that can be recycled?

Christina Chilcote, New Freedom, PA

Saving Energy

4+

LEARNING OBJECTIVES

The children will:
1. Learn about energy.
2. Learn about heat loss and electricity wastage.
3. Improve their language skills.

Materials

VOCABULARY

door	energy	save	waste
electricity	heat	shut	

WHAT TO DO

1. Talk to the children about different types of energy, particularly heat and electricity.
2. Tell the children how even small children can save energy.
3. Teach the children the following song:

Saving Energy by Anne Adeney
(Tune: "Mary, Mary, Quite Contrary")
Children, children, caring children,
Can help save energy.
Doors shut, you know,
Won't let heat go!
And we'll help save energy.

Children, children, caring children,
Can help save energy.
Turn off the light!
You know it's right!
And we'll help save energy.

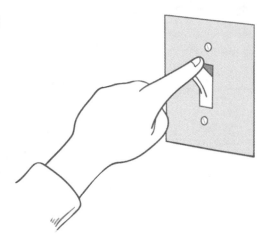

TEACHER-TO-TEACHER TIP
● Combine this song with other activities about saving energy.

ASSESSMENT
Consider the following:
● Do the children know why we need to keep doors shut in the winter?
● Do the children understand that lights are run by electricity?

Children's Books

Energy and Power by Rosie Harlow and Sally Morgan
Ready, Set, Go Green! Grades K–1 by Teresa Domnauer
Saving Energy by Charlotte Guillain

Anne Adeney, Plymouth, United Kingdom

What Can We Do?

4+

LEARNING OBJECTIVES

The children will:
1. Learn how to save water and energy.
2. Learn how to reuse and recycle.
3. Improve language skills and vocabulary.

Materials

VOCABULARY

brush	energy	morning	pass on	teeth
door	heat	packaging	recycle	work

WHAT TO DO

1. Teach the children the following song:

    What Can We Do by Anne Adeney
    (Tune: "What Shall We Do With the Drunken Sailor?")
    What can we do to care for our Earth?   What can we do to care for our Earth?
    What can we do to care for our Earth,   Every bright new morning?

    (Additional verses)
    Turn off the taps when we brush our teeth…
    Turn off the lights when we leave a room…
    Keep the doors shut when the heat is on…
    Give old things away, don't throw them out…
    Recycle packaging for something new…

2. Repeat the first line of each verse three times (two syllables on last word) and add, "every bright new morning."
3. Teach a new verse each morning. All day concentrate hard on doing (or not doing) what you have sung about.

TEACHER-TO-TEACHER TIP

- Make up simple verses to match what you are teaching.

ASSESSMENT

Consider the following:
- Ask the children one way they could save water.
- Ask the children what is the best thing to do with good clothes when we grow out of them.
- Ask the children why we need to turn off the lights when we leave a room.

> Anne Adeney, Plymouth, United Kingdom

Children's Books

Let's Save Water by Sara E. Nelson
Let's Turn It All Off by Alison Reynolds
Let's Use It Again by Alison Reynolds

Our Earth

5+

LEARNING OBJECTIVES

The children will:
1. Develop their memorization skills.
2. Think of ways to care for the Earth.

Materials

poster board
marker

VOCABULARY

bear	breathe	Earth	home	snake
bee	butterfly	everyone	recycle	sun
birds	conservation	fish		

PREPARATION
- Print "Our Earth" poem on poster board.

WHAT TO DO
1. Set out a poster board with the copy of the following poem on it, and read the poem with the children:

1. Turn out the lights.
2. Recycle.
3. Reuse old things to make something new
4. Pick up trash.
5. Don't be a litter bug.

Our Earth by Kathryn Hake
The Earth is home to birds and fish,
Butterflies and bees,
Salamanders, snakes, and bears,
And people just like me.
We need to keep things clean and green
As we travel round the sun.
So we can live and eat and breathe
In this home for everyone.

2. After reading the children the poem, engage them in a discussion about the kinds of things they can do to help keep the Earth clean and green. Copy the children's suggestions onto the poster board.

ASSESSMENT
Consider the following:
- Are the children able to learn the poem?
- Can the children name ways to care for the Earth?

Children's Books

Earth Day Birthday
by Pattie Schnetzler
The Earth and I
by Frank Asch
Why Should I Recycle?
by Jen Green

Kathryn Hake, Brownsville, OR

Reduce, Reuse, Recycle

5+

LEARNING OBJECTIVES

The child will:

1. Expand their awareness of the Earth's elements, such as water, ice caps, land, animals, plants, and people.
2. Use fine motor skills to make pictures of the Earth.
3. Discuss and compare with others what happens to the Earth when people do and do not reduce, reuse, and recycle.

VOCABULARY

Antarctica	Earth	globe	landfill	plants
Artic	environment	ice caps	map	

PREPARATION

- Set the globe and images of the Earth out where the children can see them.

WHAT TO DO

1. Whenever anyone does anything that helps our Earth, break into song. Celebrate taking care of our Earth.

   Reduce, Reuse, Recycle by Sandra Nagel
   (Tune: "Three Blind Mice")
   Reduce, reuse, recycle.
   Reduce, reuse, recycle.
   Reduce, reuse, recycle.
   Reduce, reuse, recycle.
   Our Mother Earth we love her so.
   Our Mother Earth we love her so.
   Reduce, reuse, recycle.
   Reduce, reuse, recycle.

2. Set out the butcher paper and give each child two large paper circles.
3. Set out the rest of the materials and encourage each child to make one version of the Earth based on what it would look like if everyone recycled and another based on what the Earth would look like if no one recycled.

ASSESSMENT

Consider the following:

- Do the children appreciate the importance of caring for the Earth by recycling?
- Ask the children to describe the two different versions of the Earth they've drawn.

Sandra Nagel, White Lake, MI

Materials

globe
pictures of the Earth (rivers, landscapes, and so on)
butcher paper
crayons or markers
paper circles (2 per child)
glue and glue stick
pictures of people from all over the world
magazines or clip art
small pieces of trash: plastic, paper fliers, and newspaper

Children's Books

Don't Throw It Away! by JoAnne Nelson
Reduce, Reuse, Recycle by Rozanne Lanczak Williams
Where Does the Garbage Go? by Paul Showers

Turn It Off!

LEARNING OBJECTIVES

The children will:

1. Learn the importance of saving electricity.
2. Learn to follow directions.
3. Understand what it means to conserve electricity.

Materials

3 lamps
fan
radio
fluorescent
   lightbulb
regular lightbulb
picture of a living
   room and
   kitchen (cut from
   a magazine)

VOCABULARY

conserve	electricity	fan	off	radio
electric	energy	lights	on	

PREPARATION

● Display the radio, fan, and three lamps at the front of the classroom.

WHAT TO DO

1. Turn on the lamps, fan, and radio sitting out at the front of the classroom. Show the children how each one is plugged into an electrical outlet.
2. Recite the following rhyme with the children:

   Turn It Off! by Mary J. Murray
   Turn it off.   *When you leave the room,* (clap, clap)
   Save electricity.   *Turn it off!!* (louder)

3. Whenever it is time to move from one activity to another, invite five children (or the appropriate number of children) to stand near the five electric items and ask the all children to chant the rhyme.
4. After the children shout the final line, "Turn it off!" they should turn off the items, one by one, as they count down from five to one.
5. After the countdown, invite the children to applaud the five children for conserving energy.
6. Have the children quietly line up behind the five leaders and prepare to move on to a new activity.

ASSESSMENT

Consider the following:

● Can the children look at a set of objects and determine which are electric and which are not?
● Looking at photographs of rooms in a home, can the children identify the items that use electricity?

Mary J. Murray, Mazomanie, WI

Children's Books

Building a Green Community by Ellen Rodger
Earth Friends at Home by Francine Galko
Earth Smart by Leslie Garrett
Let's Turn It All Off by Alison Reynolds

Index of Children's Books

Index

ISBN 978-0-87659-128-4
Gryphon House / 11500 / PB

ISBN 978-0-87659-126-0
Gryphon House / 11001 / PB

ALSO AVAILABLE

ISBN 978-0-87659-088-1
Gryphon House / 13467 / PB

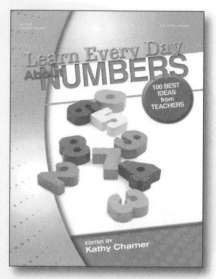

ISBN 978-0-87659-090-4
Gryphon House / 15573 / PB

ISBN 978-0-87659-092-8
Gryphon House / 16247 / PB

ISBN 978-0-87659-013-3
Gryphon House / 13614 / PB

ISBN 978-0-87659-237-3
Gryphon House / 13963 / PB

ISBN 978-0-87659-238-0
Gryphon House / 14964 / PB

ISBN 978-0-87659-285-4
Gryphon House / 18595 / PB

LEARN EVERY DAY ABOUT OUR GREEN EARTH

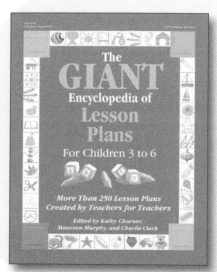

ISBN 978-0-87659-068-3
Gryphon House / 18345 / PB

ISBN 978-0-87659-166-6
Gryphon House / 19216 / PB

ISBN 978-0-87659-012-6
Gryphon House / 15002 / PB

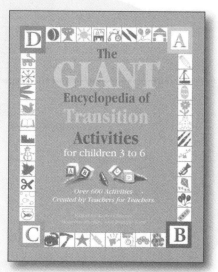

ISBN 978-0-87659-003-4
Gryphon House / 12635 / PB

ISBN 978-0-87659-001-0
Gryphon House / 11325 / PB

ISBN 978-0-87659-181-9
Gryphon House / 16413 / PB

ISBN 978-0-87659-044-7
Gryphon House / 16948 / PB

ISBN 978-0-87659-193-2
Gryphon House / 18325 / PB

ISBN 978-0-87659-209-0
Gryphon House / 16854 / PB